Praise for *She Believed She Could*

"Allison Walsh is an inspiring example and a powerful guide for anyone looking to maximize their potential and achieve their dreams. *She Believed She Could* empowers readers to overcome obstacles and create the life they truly want. Read it and achieve abundant success!"

—Rory Vaden,
cofounder of Brand Builders Group and *New York Times* best-selling author of *Take the Stairs*

"In *She Believed She Could*, Allison Walsh combines her personal journey with powerful tools and strategies to help you unlock your potential and achieve success in all areas of your life. Her authenticity, wisdom, and passion for empowering others shine through every page of this book. I highly recommend it to anyone who wants to live a fulfilling and purposeful life."

—JJ Virgin,
CNS, CHFS, celebrity nutrition and fitness expert;
four-time *New York Times* best-selling author

"Through each chapter in *She Believed She Could*, Allison guides you through making meaningful shifts in your life and career in order to fully embrace who you are. It's a perfect book for those who are ready for more in their lives and careers, and want to build their brands and businesses with intention and purpose."

—Lisa Nichols,
best-selling author; CEO,
Motivating the Masses, Inc.

"*She Believed She Could* will help you increase your confidence, develop an impactful personal brand, and create a plan for achieving success on your own terms. If you're ready for more opportunities in your life and career, this is a must-read!"

—Selena Soo,
publicity and marketing strategist

"*She Believed She Could* will help build your confidence, give you a clear road map for success, and help you build your personal brand to attract meaningful opportunities for your future. It's a must-read for anyone who is ready to be intentional about their success."

—Heather Monahan,
keynote speaker, best-selling author

"In *She Believed She Could*, Allison teaches you how to unapologetically create the life and career you've always wanted. I appreciate her sharing how she's juggled scaling businesses and raising a family, while simultaneously leaning into her passions to create a fulfilling life."

—Suneera Madhani,
founder of Stax and CEO of School

"Allison holds nothing back in *She Believed She Could* as she shares the strategies she's used to help others maximize their potential and achieve success. She provides real-life examples and helpful advice that you can immediately apply to help you become the best version of yourself that you can be."

—Carter Barnhart,
cofounder and CEO of Charlie Health

"Women leaders face unique external and internal challenges in obstacles on a path to personal and professional success. Allison's book brings together her decades of C-Suite leadership experience, positive psychology, and sisterly straight talk to give you a path forward to imposter syndrome, facing fear, and defining success on your own terms."

—Dr. Romie Mushtaq, MD;
founder of brainSHIFT;
chief wellness officer, Evolution Hospitality

"If you need a dose of positivity, some real encouragement, and incredible inspiration from a mentor who walks her talk, look no further than Allison Walsh. In *She Believed She Could*, Allison uses positive psychology and success strategies that will help you unlock your passion and purpose. After reading this book, you'll no longer dim your light and will cultivate the confidence to live your life by design."

—Gina DeVee,
author of *The Audacity to be Queen* and
founder of *Divine Living*

"As a psychologist, I know how important it is to create a compelling narrative that is honest and authentic. Allison Walsh delivers that with this book. If anyone embodies the perception of perfection from the outside, it's Allison Walsh. She is intelligent, gorgeous, ambitious, family-oriented, and generous. And in this book, she lets you in to the real, human challenges that she has worked to overcome in order to create aligned success for herself and people around her. This is the birthplace of inspiration—where authenticity and ambition meet. I'm honored to know Allison and I highly recommend this book for anyone who has wondered, 'Does this journey of life feel hard for anybody else?' She'll ignite that spark of inspiration in you to be who you want to be while enjoying the journey."

—Dr. Laura Gallaher,
CEO at Gallaher Edge and former NASA psychologist

"Allison has always been dedicated to excellence, eagerly helping others while sharing her challenges and serving as an exemplary role model. Through the years, she's encouraged thousands to achieve success, feel their best, and enjoy creating and reaching their goals. I'm sure EVERYONE reading *She Believed She Could* will be inspired by her proven strategies and principles to become enthusiastically motivated to reach both professional and personal objectives, unleashing their full potential with complete confidence."

—Lisa Maile,
professional speaker and image/communications coach

"Allison Walsh's *She Believed She Could* is a powerful reminder that we can all achieve great things. Hearing her personal journey and practical strategies provides a road map for anyone seeking to overcome their limiting beliefs and achieve their goals. This book will help you embrace your strengths and push yourself to show up daily—ready to succeed in all areas of your life."

—Cynthia Johnson,
author of *Platform: The Art and Science of Personal Branding*

"In *She Believed She Could*, Allison takes you on a powerful and beautiful journey as she shares how you can lean into your passion, purpose, and lived experiences to create a meaningful life. She'll introduce you to the world of positive psychology and how to integrate it into your life and career as she supports you to intentionally create the success you've always dreamed of."

—Niyc Pidgeon,
award-winning positive psychologist, MSc;
best-selling Hay House author of *Now Is Your Chance*; and
founder of Positive Psychology Coach Academy Certification

"Allison Walsh is an innovative and highly-successful leader in the mental health field, as well as a sought-after executive coach, speaker and consultant. Her new book, *She Believed She Could*, is terrific. It espouses proven, research-based principles to achieve success and happiness. I have personally benefitted from most of the principles in her book. It will be very valuable to anyone who is beginning their career, seeking to accelerate their progress, or considering a change in direction."

—Kim Lopdrup,
former CEO of Red Lobster

"Allison is truly an inspiration to everyone she crosses paths with. As a leader, a mentor, and a powerhouse in both the for-profit and non-profit worlds, she truly finds her "zone of genius" with this book. Allison enourages the reader by giving them the strategies to stop standing in their own way, the necessary tools to do the hard things, and the confidence to believe in themselves, each and every step of the way."

—Johanna Kandel,
CEO & Founder, National Alliance for Eating Disorders

SHE
BELIEVED
SHE
COULD

SHE BELIEVED SHE COULD

Show Up, Shine Bright, and Achieve Abundant Success

ALLISON WALSH

WILEY

Published by John Wiley & Sons, Inc., Hoboken, New Jersey.
Published simultaneously in Canada.

For general information on our other products and services or for technical support, please contact
our Customer Care Department within the United States at (800) 762-2974, outside the United States
at (317) 572-3993 or fax (317) 572-4002.

Wiley also publishes its books in a variety of electronic formats. Some content that appears in print
may not be available in electronic formats. For more information about Wiley products, visit our web
site at www.wiley.com.

Library of Congress Cataloging-in-Publication Data:

Names: Walsh, Allison, author.
Title: She believed she could : show up, shine bright, and achieve abundant
    success / Allison Walsh.
Description: Hoboken, NJ : Wiley, [2023] | Includes index.
Identifiers: LCCN 2023023692 (print) | LCCN 2023023693 (ebook) | ISBN
    9781394174300 (cloth) | ISBN 9781394174324 (adobe pdf) | ISBN
    9781394174317 (epub)
Subjects: LCSH: Positive psychology. | Success in business.
Classification: LCC BF204.6 .W35 2023 (print) | LCC BF204.6 (ebook) | DDC
    150.19/88—dc23/eng/20230707
LC record available at https://lccn.loc.gov/2023023692
LC ebook record available at https://lccn.loc.gov/2023023693

Cover Design: Wiley
Cover Images: © phochi/Shutterstock, © JF4/Shutterstock
Author Photo: Grace with Fire Photography

SKY10051755_072423

To Madison, Brooklyn, and Bradley: shine brightly, my loves.
May you chase big dreams and always believe in
your ability to achieve them.

Contents

Preface

My heart is full as I think about you reading this book. It's been a dream of mine for nearly 20 years to put these words on paper, and I'm honored that you're about to embark on this journey with me. The truth is, I would have given anything to have a book like this as I navigated the various stages of life and business, and as a result, I poured my heart and soul into these pages, sharing lessons learned the hard way, and advice I wish I would have known as I piloted opportunities and experienced setbacks.

You may be wondering, "Is this book for me?" and my hope is as you continue on, that your answer is a resounding yes! Nothing fills up my cup more than connecting with others and conveying that you are seen, valued, heard, and most of all, not alone. For so many years, I felt like I had to figure it out on my own, but the reality is, that's not the case. You are surrounded by support, and there are people out there, like me, who want nothing more than to help you succeed. One of my biggest goals is helping you understand your potential and your role in capturing it. I can believe in you 1,000%, but that won't make a difference if you don't believe in yourself. The title of this book is particularly meaningful to me, not only because it captures the importance and impact of believing in yourself but also because my daughter helped me choose the name, first for my podcast and now for this book.

I wrote this book for multi-passionate, purpose-driven individuals who are seeking confirmation that, when life is lived with intention and action, the best is yet to come. It's for the younger generation who haven't quite defined how they want to show up and need transparent advice from someone who took uncomfortable action and figured it out the hard way. It's for those who have achieved success and yet still feel unfulfilled and want more. It's for the seasoned executive who is ready to step out on their own and put all of their years of experience to work for them, instead of working for someone else. It's for those who need a reminder to get out of their own way, see what they're capable of, and finally go after what they truly want.

My story is full of examples of how to lean into your why, even when it's hard, and create brands, businesses, careers, and opportunities that are intrinsically fulfilling. Most important, it's about giving yourself permission to thrive and show up fully to reap the greatest rewards.

By leveraging decades of experience scaling businesses and personal brands, I've developed important principles for optimizing human potential. Drawing on lived experiences and positive psychology, the science of well-being, happiness, and success, I'll teach you how to level up your confidence, mindset, and vision so you can truly maximize your potential and unapologetically go after even more amazing opportunities for your future. By leaning on the science of positive psychology, I'll enhance your perspective on how to design a career and life that supports who you want to be. Each chapter encourages you to evaluate whether you are playing small versus shining brightly and gives you the game-changing tools, tips, and resources to help you optimize your potential and shine bright.

I've broken down the book into three parts, enabling you to really focus on learning and applying as we go. Part I, "Show Up," is all about embracing who you are and letting go of what's no longer in alignment with who you want to be. Part II, "Shine

Bright," is dedicated to enriching your mindset and self-confidence by evaluating who you are, how you're currently showing up in the world, and who you're surrounding yourself with. Part III, "Achieve Abundant Success," dives into defining where you're headed by giving you a rock-solid game plan and structure to rely on while teaching you how to amplify your impact, build your brand, and increase your momentum as you go after opportunities that are in alignment with who you want to be.

The message woven throughout this book is when you are intentional about who you are and what you want, and when you have done the work to create a clear brand that attracts the right people, positions, and paychecks, you will maximize your ability to share your gifts with the world and have an impact on others in ways you can't even imagine yet. The best part is, with every intentional step forward, you gain momentum, shine brighter, and become more confident and resilient so that your faith in yourself overpowers any fear you may face.

It's difficult to shine brightly these days when we're facing negativity, imposter syndrome, lack of confidence, fear, and burn-out, and my hope is that this book helps you give yourself permission to unapologetically evolve into the complete person you truly want to be. My intention is to help you go farther, progress faster, and build the confidence needed to truly evolve into the person you're meant to be.

My goal is that after reading this book you truly believe that you can do and become anything you want to be. When you believe you can, you'll discover a road map to become happier, healthier, and wealthier than before, and your mindset will be enriched. Each and every one of us has been blessed with gifts, talents, and abilities that were meant to be shared. My hope for you is to eliminate barriers and limiting beliefs so you can embrace what you bring to the table and amplify your light in life and your career in the most beautiful and authentic way. Ultimately, my mission is to help you truly embrace that you already have what it takes.

PART

Show Up

1

Optimize Your Potential
You've Already Got What It Takes

"Let's do it again, Allison," said Lisa Maile, a longtime mentor, communication expert, and friend. "You were blessed with a voice to tell your story. You're going to change lives."

I stood at the end of a runway in her coaching studio, a bit disheveled after speaking so vulnerably about what I had just overcome, but I was willing to give telling my story another go in the hopes that I could help others.

I was 18 years old and in recovery from anorexia and bulimia after a three-and-a-half-year battle. I was on a mission to not let others travel down the same path I did and had enlisted Lisa to help me learn how to responsibly and effectively tell my story. I was deeply committed to preventing others from going through what I had, and I knew deep down inside that I could make a difference if I could put my experience into words and connect with others in need of care.

In 2001, eating disorders were still highly stigmatized and there were a lot of misconceptions floating around that needed to be eradicated. In fact, a major bump in the road as I took the brave steps to get help was that those around me didn't fully understand the disease or what needed to happen for a person to get well. This reason inspired me in a powerful way to be a voice for the voiceless who were feeling super alone on their journey, just like I had felt for many years.

The decision to use my voice and own my story was one of the best decisions I ever made in my life, and it has opened more doors than I can count. After those brave days of learning to share, I started a nonprofit, Helping Other People Eat (HOPE), to raise funds for the cause. I launched the Junior Board for the National Eating Disorders Association (NEDA), a group of young advocates from across the country who wanted to mobilize efforts for the next generation of changemakers. Eventually, I transitioned to serve as the youngest member on the board of directors for NEDA for many years. I partnered with amazing organizations like the National Alliance for Eating Disorders Awareness and eventually merged my nonprofit into theirs after 18 years of running it independently. I traveled and spoke around the country and created innovative campaigns that not only focused on eating disorder prevention and treatment but also on body image, self-esteem, and confidence.

Five years later when I won Miss Florida and had the privilege to live out a lifelong dream of competing at Miss America, awareness and prevention of eating disorders was my cause of choice, and I was able to share my passion with tens of thousands of people during my year of service. All of this was possible because I didn't hide from my past or run away from my mess. In fact, I did the opposite. I leaned in, owned who I was, and allowed myself to show up fully as who I truly am. Not only was it liberating but also it was massively empowering. By sharing my story consistently and giving back daily, I built a personal brand reputation that I was really proud of. The more vocal and visible I was, the more momentum I gained, and my ability to affect lives increased substantially.

One day in 2012, I received a call from a woman who had booked me to speak several years prior. She asked if I knew anyone who would be interested in joining their team on the marketing and business development side of the treatment industry. I was fascinated by this role and said yes to this opportunity to help others in a different capacity than I had been, plus I was a third-year law student who had *zero* intention of practicing law and decided that this was a much-preferred career path.

I made the decision to enter the treatment industry and work alongside the brilliant minds working on eating disorders, addiction, and mental health treatment. A year later, I joined Advanced Recovery Systems, a start-up health care company, as employee number two, and I led the business development and branding efforts for the organization. ARS now has over 1,000 team members dedicated to changing and saving lives; operate in seven states with several additional locations under construction; and have launched a comprehensive mental wellness app, Nobu, to help enrich mental wellness. Advanced Recovery Systems is full of passionate, purpose-driven people who love what they do, further demonstrating that meaning, purpose, and leaning into your calling is a powerful path to follow. I was able to effectively turn my mess into my message and create a personal brand that has enabled me to serve in more ways than I ever imagined, opening unbelievable doors for my career and life. I'm here to tell you that you can totally do this, too. (And no, a mess is not required in order to build a beautiful brand and make a massive impact in the lives of those you serve.)

Ever since my time as Miss Florida, I've been fascinated with how building my brand created unbelievable opportunities, and I have wanted to help others do it, too. Since 2008, I've owned and operated multiple coaching and consulting companies whose bread and butter revolved around personal brand building. For many years, I focused on young women, setting them up for significant success early on in life. But in 2015, I expanded my reach because the same methodology and process were working, regardless of generation or gender.

As I got serious about writing a book, a dream of mine since I was 18 years old, I gave a lot of thought to where I could help you the most. I reflected on the journey I've been on personally with so many others and mapped out the "what I wish I had knowns" so that you can have a much smoother experience. In all honesty, I would have given anything to have my hands on a book like this, especially during the seasons when the doubts and fears were louder than my self-belief or confidence. I would have embraced the stories and appreciated the expression of vulnerability, knowing that I could do anything as long as I took uncomfortable action through brave personal decisions and bold professional moves while shedding the fear associated with fully leaning into what I truly wanted my life and career to look like. I would have loved this on the days that I wanted to give up because building companies and a family simultaneously was hard (especially during a recession, a pandemic, and another recession). Figuring things out was exhausting. Most important, I would have cherished having relatable stories that could have given me permission to go "all in" rather than playing small with my potential. I wrote this book to help you adopt a permanent mindset shift while learning to love and honor yourself each and every day as you chase and accomplish your goals. My hope is that you play full out in business and life, and fulfill your dreams, while also inspiring others to pursue theirs.

Optimize and Believe in Yourself

I always have, and always will have a soft spot in my heart for helping individuals elevate themselves and reach their fullest potential. I've been honored to work with amazing mentors, coaches, and consultants over the course of my career who have poured into me, helping me realize what else I am capable of. In times when the self-doubt was louder than the faith in myself, I was able to borrow the confidence of others as I made moves and took risks that I wasn't fully certain would work out. I am committed to doing the same for as many people as possible, which is one of the many reasons I am writing this book.

I consider every one of my clients and every member of my community to be completely capable of accomplishing what they set their minds to, meaning a person who owns who they are, looks for opportunities to shine brighter, and believes in themselves enough to chase after a new level as they build confidence and momentum along the way.

I am so incredibly excited that you are here now, too.

My number one goal is to help you realize how truly phenomenal you are and go after the goals and dreams that you have for your future. After all, regardless of whatever your official title is, you are the leader of your life and it's time to take full ownership of how you show up in this ever-changing world. Plus, the groundwork you lay and the moves you make will set you up for success in ways that may seem unimaginable. Trust that the work that you do to optimize your potential will yield results that might not even be on your radar yet.

Simply opening the cover and jumping into this book shows that you're ready for more and are open to new and exciting possibilities for your future. You are capable of anything you set your mind to, and I am here to help you get there. It's time to leverage who you are, get visible, amplify your influence, and attract incredible opportunities. Success doesn't happen by accident, and I don't take this responsibility lightly. My intention is to serve up exactly what you need to level up in business and life.

Throughout this book, I'll help you uncover areas that can be optimized for you to be able to show up with confidence, own every aspect of who you are, and assist you in achieving abundant success because you were willing to stop playing small and lean into who you were truly meant to be.

Nothing is worse than untapped potential, yet millions of people struggle to fully maximize their gifts, talents, abilities, and possibilities each and every day. Even worse, it's really easy to passively subscribe to playing small by allowing ourselves to stay stuck in a place, space, or version of our identity to which we no longer belong.

At the end of the day, doubt will kill more dreams than failure ever will. Whether it's a lack of clarity, uncertainty about how to pursue your dreams, fear of failure or what other people will think, or the self-doubt saboteur showing up, we've got to stop it in its tracks so you can play full out in this game of life and live on purpose with purpose.

If you're feeling overwhelmed already, please pause and hear me out. There are incredible tools and resources available in this book that I've used and shared over the last 20 years that can help elevate your mindset; get crystal clear about your unique talents and strengths; design a life filled with happiness, joy, and success; and build a brand that you're super proud of so you can go after whatever opportunities you want in life and business. Hundreds of my one-on-one clients have used these lessons as I've walked alongside them, supporting them as they've committed to their goals and made massive action happen in their lives and careers. I've used them as I've coached multimillion-dollar teams as they've started and scaled businesses and brands. And I've inspired thousands of ambitious dream chasers in my community to go for it, whatever it may be, by trusting the principles in this book. I am here to help you do the same, and I could not be more honored to have the opportunity to enrich your life, open your eyes to possibilities, give you the tools you need to make moves, and help you achieve the outcomes you've desired as you truly own who you are and show up fully to claim what's yours.

Throughout each page of this book, I'll guide you through evaluating core areas of your life and career that can benefit from an intentional audit of where you are versus where you want to be so that you align all of your intentions and actions to yield the best results. I'll also share behind-the-scenes stories that will reinforce the principles and provide some humor along the way.

As I look around today, I see so much professional discontent—people working hard, but without true purpose, passion, or fulfillment. I see incredible people waiting for permission to go all in rather than building their brand and confidence along the way so that they attract aligned opportunities for their future. I see way too many individuals operating on autopilot rather than taking control of the steering wheel. That needs to stop, and the only way to do so is to be super intentional about our next steps.

Collectively, we've all been through a lot. Like it or not, none of us are the same person we were pre-pandemic. Our eyes have been opened. Our perspectives have changed. The possibilities for the future are different than what we thought they would be, and there's likely some switching, changing, and rearranging that we could benefit from. Now, more than ever, we need to look within ourselves, leverage who we are, and go after what we want, rather than letting anyone or anything else dictate our outcomes.

Positive Psychology Will Change Your Life and Career

Optimizing your potential can sound like a daunting process, but there are tools and strategies that can help you approach it. The framework I use is based on positive psychology, a field dedicated to the study of human flourishing. It provides you with key concepts and principles that can help you break out of survival mode and live a more meaningful and fulfilling life. They will help you tap into your potential and act on it, enabling you to optimize your life.

Although I have been blessed to have unbelievable training, coaching, and mentorship since I was a teenager, this most recent exposure had a profound impact on my life and the trajectory of my career. Its refreshing perspective and universal concepts have the ability to transform the lives of anyone who chooses to adopt them, and I truly believe that these principles, coupled with leadership, business, and brand building concepts woven together, will help you achieve abundant success and happiness however you choose to apply them. Here's a brief overview of each pillar before we jump into them deeper throughout the book (see Figure 1.1).

- **Positive emotions:** Boost your resilience with the right balance of positive emotions. Learn how to reduce stress, navigate your emotions, and diffuse overwhelm.
- **Engagement:** Increase your confidence and creativity by learning how to leverage your unique neurological skills and intrinsic values to unlock your full potential in your personal life and professional life.

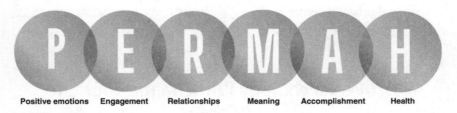

FIGURE 1.1 The principles of positive psychology.

- **Relationships.** Create meaningful relationships with your-self and others by allowing yourself to feel loved, connected, and supported as you work on your next level.

- **Meaning.** Discover your purpose in life, embrace your call-ing, and create a sense of connection to something bigger than yourself without overextending yourself or burning out.

- **Accomplishment.** Lean into your ability to do the things that matter most to you and bring you the greatest fulfill-ment personally and professionally while developing a growth mindset to unlock your full potential.

- **Health.** Maximize your energy and radiance by creating sustainable healthy habits that enhance your physical and psychological health and your ability to consistently show up as the best version of yourself.

It's my intention that these pillars, coupled with the princi-ples shared throughout the book, the lessons I've chosen to share, and the additional frameworks that I've used to coach and train ambitious, motivated individuals over the last two decades, will help you identify areas in your life in which you could and should lean into in order to maximize your success.

And while I believe in you 1,000%, my goal is for you to have the same level of self-confidence within yourself. But full disclo-sure before we begin: if I want this more for you than you want this for yourself, we have a problem.

You'll quickly learn that I live and die by a mentality of being 1% better, meaning that if you commit to being just 1% better today than you were yesterday, and you stay consistently committed to yourself,

Commit to being just 1% better today and you will make incredible things happen.

you will make incredible things happen. Plus, you'll gain momentum and results as you put yourself to the test, and quitting or canceling on yourself will no longer be an option.

If you're reading this book, chances are you've read other business, self-help, and personal development books. Kudos to you because you're already separating yourself from the crowd. You're committed to learning more, doing more, and exploring what else exists for your future. Although many books introduce principles that have a familiar flavor, I'm adding a new twist by using the pillars of positive psychology to help you apply the concepts in your life. The exercises in each chapter will help you appreciate how exceptional you are, how you can leverage your uniqueness, and how to build your brand to attract incredible opportunities for your future.

I've always been super curious about how the world's most inspiring and successful people do the things they do. I consider myself a pretty motivated and disciplined person and have implemented many solid foundational practices to help me get to where I am today. I'm sure this is a major reason why I gravitated toward the teachings of positive psychology and why I am so excited to share them with you, too. The best part about it is that with simple, subtle shifts, you can make massive changes in your life and truly step into your full potential, thus increasing your confidence every step of the way. The pillars will raise your level of self-awareness, which can be a transformative experience in and of itself, helping you to really understand who you are, how to leverage your talents and strengths, and weave them into a game plan for your future. The beautiful part is that these principles can also be immediately applied to your career, enabling you to truly maximize your potential and create a brand you're proud of.

I truly believe that the whole point of being alive is to evolve into the complete person you were intended to be. My mission is to ignite the flame within you to know that you are 1,000% capable of creating the life and career you want, even if it still seems like a dream. My hope is that you are so lit up on the inside after reading this book that you start to make the moves you need to in order to truly create the career, business, and life of your dreams. I'll give you what you need to navigate your own journey and show up every day with the "be amazing" mentality. It's not just about managing life; it's about giving yourself permission to thrive, flourish, and optimize your potential each and every day, and shine a spotlight on who you are so you can make an even bigger difference in this world. My hope is that you walk away with a "permission granted" mentality and are ready to amplify your impact, live intentionally, celebrate who you are, and create an epic life for yourself.

And as a reminder for you like the one I received back in 2001: you were blessed with talents, gifts, abilities, and a voice to tell your story. You're going to change lives and inspire people you don't even know simply by showing up, shining your light, and sharing who you are with the world. Anything is possible if you're willing to give yourself the time and energy you deserve.

Buckle up, because it's your turn to do what you believe you can. I know the world will be a much better place once you embrace how truly spectacular you are and allow yourself to dream bigger than ever before.

2

Own It
Embrace Who You Are

Similar to many other people, I struggled to find my true path and purpose early on in my career. When I graduated from college and moved to Miami, I had a terrible time finding a job and started to get very concerned about my future. After a year of coaching baton-twirling students for a local studio to pay the bills, I knew I needed to make moves. I signed up and took the law school admissions test on the same day as I auditioned to compete for Miss Miami. Ultimately, I ended up going to law school years later because it seemed like the next best choice, and something that many other people were excited about. In the story of my life, it turns out that my JD stood more for "just delaying" than Juris doctorate, and I learned a challenging and very expensive lesson.

It didn't take me long to realize that I was on the wrong path, but I am a stubborn human at times and pride myself on finishing what I start. I was also extremely concerned about disappointing the people in my circle who were really excited that I was going to be an attorney. Adding an interesting twist to the equation, the recession was rocking our worlds while I was in school, and my husband lost his job five months after we said, "I do." Our savings were draining quickly and in many ways, my access to student loans was helping to keep us afloat while I figured out what to do next. The more entrenched I became with the study of law and the real-world experiences I was having through internships and my mentors, the more I realized that this was not the right path. The problem was I still wasn't sure what I should do next.

As an attempt to generate joy and cash flow during a season of feeling lost, I started a coaching company. Coaches had always had an incredible impact on my outcomes, and I wanted to be able to do the same for others. I kept it simple and coached out of our living room on most days, and had special clients who soaked up my advice. It turned out that I really loved being able to pour into young women and help them reach their goals. There's a common saying that you are best positioned to help the client you once were, so for me, that meant young women in the Miss America Organization. It enabled me to leverage my strengths, share past experiences, help them realize what they were capable of, create a plan to accomplish it, and make it happen. Winner after winner, my love for this continued to grow. I leaned into it more each season, expanding my list of clientele, and learned better ways to get the most out of each young woman I worked with. Having something that gave me so much happiness also made it easier to manage law school, which for me, left me with the opposite feelings.

I wasn't the type of pageant coach that just focused on walking, wardrobe, and talking; rather, I focused on building the brand of each young woman I worked with. They were ambitious, hard-working, and focused, and with enough gentle pushes, I could help them step outside of their comfort zones and start believing in their own potential. We had deadlines, which I loved because we were able to create success timelines and get a lot accomplished in a short period of time. We focused on executive presence, confidence building, and strong communication skills, which were foundational elements that would help them far beyond their pageant days. I am fascinated by high performers and this opportunity let me influence the next generation who were highly focused on making a difference in this world while helping them create a foundation for themselves that would set them up for success regardless of their path in the future. Because of the work we did, they were getting to really know themselves and own their magnificence early in life, which made a massive difference in how they showed up and when they were stacked among their peers. Watching them succeed and open doors they never thought possible was so incredibly special, and I am grateful for each and every client whom I had the privilege to work with. It gave me the chance to invest time, energy, and resources into talented humans who really enjoyed the process. It also enabled me to create a curriculum that would later evolve to serve even more clients in a future iteration of the business.

During that season of life, and despite the fact that we were struggling to bounce back from the recession while I was simultaneously accumulating tens of thousands of dollars in student loan debt, I came clean to my family that law was not going to be my chosen career path. I had to have brave conversations that created more anxiety leading up to them than they were worth. And although I had gained a newfound respect for lawyers and what it takes to be one, I had no intention of joining that profession. I knew it was a letdown, but it was also me standing in my truth once again, being honest with what wasn't going right, and unsubscribing from something that I knew was not for me. Looking back, I am really proud of that decision. Plus, dipping my toes in the entrepreneurial waters through coaching helped me to recognize other possibilities for sharing my gifts and talents with the world, and I was eager to figure out how to do more of that. I was fascinated by the fact that my lived experiences at this stage of my life were incredibly valuable and could generate significant cash flow by me monetizing my knowledge base and sharing the lessons I had learned with clients who wanted to walk in the same footsteps and have similar opportunities.

From the business perspective, I knew there was more potential, but I was already wearing too many crowns as it was. In order to really scale, I needed a new business plan or model that would enable substantial growth. As I was wrapping up law school, I was also working in the mental health treatment industry in a new capacity beyond the nonprofit organization I had run for so long, and I was a new mom to our beautiful daughter, Madison. I cared deeply about the community I was serving through the nonprofit and wasn't ready to completely walk away just yet. And although I wanted to cannonball into the pageant-coaching business pool, I didn't want to do it alone. I worried about failure and what others would think, so I avoided leaning into my calling a bit further until I was able to, yet again, find "my brave" and go for it.

Choosing to Own It

"Pass the wine," I said. It was a typical Sunday night at the McKenna household, filled with beverages, tacos, and friendship.

Jennifer McKenna had quickly become one of my besties while we were both working at Miss America's Outstanding Teen prior to my going to law school. She's driven, loves to get things done, and subscribes to a "why not?" mentality. She's also a former Miss Virginia and a coach like me, so we always had tons to talk about. Plus, we had dabbled in a photography business for a while so what was about to transpire shouldn't have been a shock to either of us. I was the yin to her yang and we loved doing things together.

Tijuana Flats take-out was our favorite go-to on a Sunday night, and talking shop was always a good time. However, this particular chat led in a new direction that neither of us was expecting. "What if we merged our coaching businesses?" I said. "We can get them out of our homes, into a studio, and create something really special." To say our husbands liked the constant flow of clients in and out of our homes would be a lie. Plus, we were both moms at this point and needed separation between home life and business.

"Yes" was her immediate response, and the rest of the evening was spent brainstorming. For the next several weeks we were consumed by the thought of going all in, putting the necessary formalities in place, and creating a vision for what we wanted our studio to be.

Jennifer found the *perfect* studio location. We borrowed $10,000 to do what we needed to do to make it a one-of-a-kind experience by creating a full-service coaching and professional management studio and never looked back. That decision rocked our worlds, and let me tell you: the Universe delivered *big time*. It was crazy how fast everything happened and looking back it's such a good reminder that when you're in alignment with your energy and what you're good at, magic will happen.

We presold packages and paid back our loan instantly, and before we knew it we crossed the six-figure revenue mark. We monetized the heck out of that business and did things others in our space never even contemplated, most of which worked out well. Our one-on-one client list exceeded 100 in year two and their successes were incredible. We were on the covers of industry magazines and clients were flying in from all across the country to work with us in person. It was unbelievable at the time, and our girls were winning over and over and over again, so we spent nothing on advertising.

Most important, we had an absolute blast doing it. Our clients became like family and we adored the time we spent with them. What's even better is that many are still in our lives today, nearly 10 years later. Now we could have easily continued to play small with our individual businesses, but we chose to lean in, trust in our abilities, and play big, and it paid off big time. And, yes, we worked our buns off to make it amazing, but when you love what you're doing, who you're doing it with, and are lit up on the inside, it's a totally different experience than working long days and nights doing something that you hate.

It was during this same season of life that the phone rang with opportunities to expand my work in the treatment industry. After all, I had built a pretty substantial brand for myself in the mental health and eating disorder awareness and prevention world before, during, and after my year as Miss Florida, and the network I created was ripe with life-changing opportunities as a result of my commitment to the cause and desire to make a difference in this world.

A few years into our business ventures, Jennifer was pregnant with her fourth child in five years, and I was staring at a career advancement opportunity that couldn't be left unexplored. We made the decision that it was time to wind down our beautiful baby of a business and take advantage of the time to focus on what was next for both of us. I will forever look back on this time in my life and be grateful for the lessons learned. It also made me really appreciate the talents I brought to the table and provided a crystal-clear example of what's possible when you love what you do.

It Might Be Time for a Wake-Up Call

As I have continued to progress in my career and start and scale other companies, I've been exposed to so many amazing tools that I wish I would have had my fingers on back then. Really knowing who you are, what makes you happy, and knowing how to leverage who you are to help you elevate your strengths can make a significant difference in your life and career.

And although I am grateful that I woke up to the reality that staying on the legal career track was not the right move, there are millions of people who have not woken up to what "could be" for them if they were to align themselves with opportunities that would enable them to truly flourish.

Now you may feel differently, and that you're on the right track, but stay with me here. The following questions may help uncover opportunities to elevate where you are now and in the future. But, if you're feeling a bit more seen right now, as I mention discontent and lack of fulfillment, we need to pause and help you create intentional next steps to maximize your potential.

The best way to really *own* who you are now versus where you want to be in the future is to audit the story of your life and career. When we own our past and become confident in our present and who we are in this moment, we can create our future. Further, when we remove the rigid expectations of having to have it all figured out before we even get started, we give ourselves permission to explore opportunities that we might otherwise stray from. I could have easily strayed from something I loved and not pursued building McKenna Walsh, but had I done that, I would have wallowed in my misery, missed out on *so* much fun, and not learned really valuable lessons that I'll continue to share with you throughout this book. I could have allowed my worries of what other people might think to stop me in my tracks, but instead, I released their judgments and allowed myself to embrace the chance to make an impact on each of the young women's lives that walked through our doors.

Trust me when I say there were plenty of haters along the way. When Jennifer and I showed up doing what we loved, it triggered others who weren't following their dreams or those who were jealous of the success we were experiencing. We made a conscious decision to show up anyways, and instead of dimming our light, we focused on all of the good we were doing and the transformations our clients were experiencing along the way. As our girls blew their goals out of the water, we shouted from the rooftops and celebrated their successes, because, at the end of the day, they were proof of what could be done when you believe in yourself and turn dreams into plans. And although we were in the business of empowering young women, we wanted to inspire others to do the same regardless of age or gender.

You have one shot to make the most of the 1,440 minutes in each day, and my hope is that you close your eyes each night knowing that you're living the life you want to live.

It's really easy to let fear, doubt, and judgment stop you in your tracks, but I want to focus on you truly *owning* who you are and what makes you happy. This is *your* life. You have one shot to make the most of the 1,440 minutes in each day, and my hope is that you close your eyes each night knowing that you're living the life *you* want to live. I want to empower you to really look in the mirror and decide if what you are doing now is filling up your cup the way you want it to.

You Deserve to Be Fulfilled

When I started diving into the research of positive psychology, it became so clear why I enjoyed this adventure so much. Not only was the meaning pillar activated because I loved helping young women realize their potential and there's long-standing research behind the benefits of mentorship for both the mentee and mentor. It also enabled me to tap into the engagement pillar by leveraging my strengths in a way that I wasn't fully aware of at the time.

In positive psychology, the engagement pillar helps you embrace the concept of flow theory. It's intended to help you create as many opportunities as possible to do work that is so fulfilling that you lose track of time, while simultaneously challenging and inspiring you. It encourages you to really evaluate how, when, and where you are the most engaged on a day-to-day basis and draw a line to what created that level of engagement so you can do more of what's working and less of what's not.

The engagement pillar is rooted in strengths-based coaching and self-awareness. When you know who you truly are at your core, what your neurological strengths are, and what provides you with the greatest access to tapping into those strengths every day, you can create alignment between what you want and what you need to truly thrive personally and professionally.

Positive psychology encourages you to take a ton of different assessments, which I love and hope you do, too. I was always the girl taking the quizzes in the back of the magazine, and I'll click on just about any online quiz that opens my eyes to something I didn't know before. I also really appreciate that positive psychology focuses on the elevation of your strengths rather than spending time on weaknesses, which is a natural tendency for many.

Strengths Finder, Enneagram, High-Performance Habits, Myers-Briggs, the VIA assessment, and many more are used to help raise your level of self-awareness and connect the dots between you and your potential. For a full list of recommended assessments, go to www.shebelievedbook.com/resources.

For me, there were so many "aha" moments that happened as I revisited many of the assessments that I had taken at previous times in my life. The real magic with these is when you can pause and really apply what you've learned about yourself and see the presence of each result in your life. And although there is no one-size-fits-all assessment that will resonate with every single person, there are amazing tools that, when approached with an open mindset and desire to learn, can positively affect you in countless ways.

Your Strengths Are Your Superpowers

As someone who admittedly is a "recovering perfectionist," I spent way too many hours trying to fix what wasn't good enough. Additionally, I had spent decades in the behavioral health world, again trying to fix what was wrong with those we were serving. The concept of elevating and focusing on what was "right" was liberating, and the deeper I've gone into this work with myself and others, the more I've realized the profound impact it can have on your life and career.

For me, Strengths Finder (available through Gallup[1]) further solidified why I love coaching and elevating human potential so much. The true magic was in understanding my top five and how they interact with one another, along with how my supporting strengths, those listed 6 to 10, show up to enhance my performance and outcomes. Knowing that I embody these strengths helps me have the confidence to seek out even more roles, contracts, and clients to help others become their best. I encourage you to learn more about yours as well! I've included the Gallup 34 Strengths and resources to dive deeper at www.shebelievedbook.com/resources. And although I would *love* to

---

[1] https://store.gallup.com/p/en-us/10003/cliftonstrengths-34

do a deep dive with your strengths, too (hopefully our paths will cross in the future), I'll use mine as an illustration of how to best leverage this powerful self-awareness tool.

First and foremost, there's only a 1 in 30 million chance that someone else will have the same top five, in the same order, as you. How cool is that? Now that you're hopefully feeling extra special and unique, it's time to appreciate this new level of awareness even more. The true beauty is not staying surface level. Instead, notice how your strengths show up individually and in combination with each other, and give yourself credit when you notice them helping you. They can also be used to evaluate your current responsibilities and future opportunities with the intention of finding alignment, which leads to greater fulfillment, happiness, and success (sign me up for more of that!).

To get personal, here are my five in order: strategic, futuristic, achiever, competitive, and significance. Once identified, now it's time to apply them and notice how tapping into them makes you feel. For example, in the coaching business, strategic and futuristic would get lit up whenever I was game-planning with a client. I have the ability to see the potential in people and concepts, and creating a strategy to make them happen made it so much fun. Because of the industry that my first business was focused on, achiever and competitive would play together all of the time. Significance was humming whenever I was in a position to feel really valued as a part of someone's team or that they trusted my opinion. It makes perfect sense why that business felt so rewarding and why I've continued to create other coaching and consulting businesses and thrived in the business world when I was positioned to pour into others, elevate their performance, and help them succeed.

Fast forward since closing the doors of McKenna Walsh, and I've intentionally created countless opportunities to coach, train, mentor, and speak on stages to thousands of people. See my strengths were the affirmations that elevated my desire to make this a permanent part of my day-to-day. I can wholeheartedly attest that it's when I feel the most alive, and my hope is that you find that same sense of alignment with where you spend your time and energy.

When Your Strengths Become Your Shadows

Equally important is knowing that your strengths can also be your shadows. I had the chance to learn from and be coached by organizational psychologist and leadership expert, Dr. Laura Gallaher. During our time together we did a lot of work with our team on defensiveness and how we respond and react when we are triggered. These teachings resonated deeply with me as she explained that our defenses are triggered by any one of the following challenges:

- When our likeability is at stake
- When our credibility is questioned
- When our significance is minimized

Ding! Ding! Ding! The light bulbs lit up for me as I realized that not only was significance in my top five strengths but also it was my biggest trigger when it came to being defensive. For example, if someone canceled a meeting last minute, or even worse, was really late with no notice or remorse, I would get very peeved. If ever the depth of my influence or role was minimized, my defensiveness and over-justification would show up. Through these really valuable leadership lessons with Dr. Gallaher, coupled with the positive psychology coach certification training I was undertaking simultaneously, I was able to gain a much greater awareness and understanding of what made me tick and emerged as a better leader, employee, coach, and friend. Really seeing the tea leaves, so to speak, has not only helped me know myself better but also has built my confidence in ways I couldn't have imagined prior to those experiences.

It's also been priceless when it comes to leading and coaching others because I can not only help them appreciate their strengths but also I'm able to help them be incredibly mindful of when, why, and how they show up in a negative way or are reacting to unexpected triggers for them. Being able to "name it and tame it," meaning recognizing and moving on rather than getting stuck in emotions, enhances one's executive presence, emotional intelligence, and self-awareness.

Personally, I can now check myself in a variety of ways and really tune in to what I am feeling and why. It helps me take an honest look in the mirror and better evaluate myself, the things I am involved in, and what I say yes to. I encourage you to spend time learning more about yourself so that you have your own measuring sticks, too. This can be exceptionally helpful for the recovering people pleasers or for those who might let a scarcity mindset dictate their obligations. Let it serve as a reminder to not just do the things that others want you to do or say yes because you think there might not be another opportunity (because there will be). Make sure that your yeses are in alignment with who you are and what you want. This is your life, not theirs, and there are plenty of opportunities for you, many of which you can't even see yet.

Own Your Past, Present, and Future

In addition to taking advantage of all of the tools discussed in this chapter, I highly encourage you to really evaluate your past, where you are presently, and get excited about the future. The older I've gotten and the more experience I've gained, the more I've come to realize how much more in the driver's seat we are than we give ourselves credit for.

It's really easy to blame terrible, unfortunate, or unfair situations that have occurred in our lives and use them as excuses rather than the fuel to create change. It can be way easier to repeat history than change it, and until new habits or intentions are formed and solidified (which we will also get into further on in this book) it can be more convenient to operate on autopilot and cosign on a life, career, or obligation that isn't in alignment with who we are truly meant to be.

Here's the deal. You are unique, blessed beyond measure, and special in more ways than you can fathom. You were uniquely designed to leave a legacy and owe it to yourself to fully leverage who you are at your core to make a difference in this world. You have gifts, talents, and strengths that are meant to be shared while creating a ripple effect that you can't comprehend just yet. You have the ability to change lives and make a *massive* impact on whomever you choose to serve, whether that's a company, your own clients in your business, your community, and/or your friends and family. And the best part is that it all starts with your intention to do so coupled with the belief in your ability to take what may feel like an uncomfortable step forward each and every day.

Listen and trust me when I say, you can do this and deserve to live the life you can't stop dreaming about. When you really get quiet with yourself and your thoughts (which I know can be incredibly difficult at times), you can intentionally make moves and choices that get you closer to your ideal life or career. We can't be casual about life, and when you know yourself and trust yourself, you can open doors for yourself simply by showing up as the full, most vibrant version of yourself.

You deserve to live the life you can't stop dreaming about.

In order to really own who you are, you've got to get really clear and extremely honest about yourself. You know by now that

I love to start on a high note, so first and foremost, give yourself credit for where you are right now. Truly take a step back and look at what you've done to get to where you are. Make a list of everything that it took for you to be who you are at this moment. I want you to see on paper (or a note on your phone) the work you've done to be the version of yourself that you are right now. You are amazing and you must give yourself credit for the journey thus far.

Please resist the temptation to give yourself a hard time about the past; rather, focus on the fact that you are resilient and have made it to where you are now as a result of your commitment to yourself. Chances are you've overcome a lot and you have survived 100% of your bad days. You literally cannot change the past or rewind time, so please be kind to yourself as you reflect back. Instead, I want you to focus on the strength you've gained by being you: your lived experiences, your sacrifices, and your ability to overcome things you probably didn't think you would go through have made you capable of facing whatever is next. Remember, if it doesn't challenge you, it doesn't change you, so instead of shaming the struggle, celebrate who you are today as a result of it.

If you're holding on to the past and struggling to move forward, let's flip the script. I encourage you to write out the challenging situations you've experienced and dig deep to identify how those experiences have shaped who you are today. Use Table 2.1 to complete this, then try to find at least two or three

Table 2.1 Challenges and Takeaways

Experience	What I Learned	I Am Stronger Because

takeaways, or ways to give yourself credit for moving past each experience, and give yourself credit for where you are at this moment in time.

It's pretty incredible, isn't it? We don't pause and do this nearly enough and as a result, we can end up missing out on the opportunities to celebrate our growth and development and honor our journeys. Additionally, it can be really easy to get ourselves on autopilot mode and lose track of our progress because we are so focused on the final destination that we haven't yet reached. I'm also a firm believer that expressing gratitude for the journey sends a signal that we're ready for more abundance and opportunities to flow our way.

And if you're inclined to blame your past for where you are, I need you to pause and pay attention: you are capable of starting over whenever you choose, but in order to really move forward, you have to release and let go of what's holding you back. In many cases, these can be connected to your origin stories or limiting beliefs that you've been carrying along for way too long. It's time to rewrite the stories we tell ourselves if we truly want to elevate and go after bigger goals and dreams.

I'm always reminded that some of my darkest times have ultimately led to the most meaningful moments and chances to positively affect others. Overcoming my battle with eating disorders enabled me to serve tens of thousands of people, letting them know help is available and recovery is possible. Overcoming our financial struggle when my husband lost his job and was unemployed for a year made us a stronger couple when it could have easily destroyed us. Rehiring our Advanced Recovery Systems team members after a layoff due to the pandemic was one of the most gratifying experiences of my career knowing we had worked collectively as a team to bounce back during a time of incredible uncertainty. Holding our rainbow baby for the first time after experiencing a miscarriage solidified how badly I wanted to be a mother and how grateful I was to be able to bring that dream to fruition.

Any one of those positive results (many of which took longer than I wanted) might not ever have existed if I let the initial negative experience be the end of the story. I encourage you to keep this in mind if your brain skewed to the hurt over the hope when I just asked this of you. You have the ability to rewrite the story of your life. After all, you are the author and plots twists are absolutely acceptable.

Next, I want you to be super honest with yourself. Are you where you want to be? Are you truly doing the things you want to be doing? Are you surrounded by the people you want to be around? Are you lit up on the inside at the thought of doing the work you do day in and day out? If the answer is yes, that is incredible. Keep leaning in and embracing the opportunities that provide such experiences. My mission for you is to help elevate your awareness of how to maximize your potential and see possibilities that you haven't seen before.

If the answer is no, that is 1,000% okay. Know that you are not alone, and I will pour into you throughout this book to help open your eyes to the possibilities that exist and give you a road map to follow. Give yourself credit for acknowledging your truth and let it be the first step to setting you free. Denying it will only keep you stuck in a version of yourself that you've already outgrown so get ready to grow. Your possibilities are endless.

Now I want you to really look inward and think about who you want to be in the future. What does your life look like? What does your career look like? Who do you spend time with? What have you experienced that you were once too scared to dream about? If you can't pinpoint a clear vision at the moment, it's okay. Focus on how you want to feel. What words come to mind? Free? Happy? Clear? Wealthy? Healthy? Content? Or, maybe something else that's deeply personal to you?

Take these thoughts (and hopefully the notes you've taken) with you as we continue to move throughout the book. Self-awareness truly is your superpower. Knowing yourself and being honest about what you want is one of the greatest gifts you can give yourself. My intention as we move forward is to help identify any blocks that may be in your way, give you helpful guidance on how to take care of yourself so you can live your best, most abundant life, and empower you to believe in yourself while you lean into your potential to achieve unstoppable success.

Own who you are at this moment and get really excited about the future. You deserve all of the blessings heading your way. See yourself as the magnificent person you are. Honor the journey thus far. Set *your* intentions (not anyone else's) and get prepared for what's next, because it's going to be incredible.

And as Jennifer and I said to the hundreds of clients that walked through our McKenna Walsh doors, "Don't be afraid to be amazing. You've got this."

3

Let Go to Grow
Release What's Holding You Back

I know I am not alone when it comes to having regrets, experiencing realizations late in the game, and necessary awakenings that would have been helpful months, if not years, before. As I'll share throughout this book and this chapter especially, mine always seem to happen at inopportune times, or periods where it felt like everything was happening all at once, where my faith and determination were challenged beyond what I anticipated, truly testing my commitment to the moves I was making. One of the most pivotal examples rocked my world right after graduating from college, but that singular decision and dedication to myself and what I wanted shaped my life forever.

A Necessary Change

I had been engaged to my college sweetheart for a couple of years by the time I realized that the direction I was headed was not what I wanted and the life we were destined for was not what I desired.

During my last semester of college, I moved to Miami to support my fiancé's dream while I completely neglected mine. I was allowing myself to be complacent rather than the trailblazer I had been before and during college. In the months following the move, I was constantly compromising what I wanted and dimming my light. I felt like I had lost myself and my identity between August and the following June, and the writing was clearly on the wall that there was no change, only demise, in sight. I was letting my ambitions dwindle and I was sacrificing opportunities for no clear reason other than I didn't want to lose the relationship we had despite the fact that I wasn't happy. It was incredibly clear that I was not living up to my potential regardless of the collegiate career that I had had, which should have been an exceptional springboard to post-graduation success. Instead, I wasn't making the moves I needed to in order to lay any foundation for a true career and I was more lost than ever.

Even worse, I didn't like who I had become. Bad choices. Bad influences. Bad crowd. It was becoming more and more clear that if something didn't change quickly, I would only continue to create more distance between myself and the goals and dreams I once had for myself.

For me, competitions, or anything with a deadline for that matter, forced me to get my act together, which was a major reason why I signed up to compete in the Miss Miami contest. And because I had thankfully qualified for Miss Florida 2006 by winning that local competition, I had a new deadline and was beginning to regain my motivation and focus. I knew deep down that if I didn't give it a shot, I would live with that regret for years to come and that wasn't something I was willing to do.

As the competition week of Miss Florida was getting closer and closer, it felt as though the relationship between my fiancé and me was getting more and more strained over decisions and the direction we were each headed toward, which very much seemed like it was not in alignment like it once had been.

Three weeks prior to Miss Florida week, I had hit a breaking point and somehow manufactured the courage to temporarily move out of our apartment. I crashed on the floor of a friend's house while I sorted out my thoughts and started to regain clarity about what I really wanted. After three prior attempts to win Miss Florida and the reality that my future attempts were limited due to eligibility, I had to be serious about my preparation, mindset, and focus if I actually wanted this to happen. In Miss America, there's an age limit that forces your retirement and the clock was ticking. Plus, as a competitive baton twirler who had technically already retired when I graduated from college and moved on from our national championship team, the older I got, the more difficult it was to maintain the level of athleticism and flexibility needed to perform at my best. And last, pageant or not, I knew deep down inside that something had to give and this was an opportunity to change my life for the better in a multitude of ways.

If I wanted that week to go well, I had to get myself in a better headspace, which meant that I had to let go of the version I once was to truly allow myself to become who I wanted to be. The day before I checked in to compete for Miss Florida, I asked my fiancé to meet me at the apartment before he went to work. "I don't want to marry you anymore," I told him.

Those were some of the hardest words I ever had to say 22 years into my life. He didn't understand. I was more mad than sad at that point, but we agreed to let me get through the next week at Miss Florida, and then we would sort everything else out.

I proceeded to pack up what I needed and left. Thankfully, all contestants were required to stay at the hotel not too far away, which was a welcomed reprieve.

Because it was my fourth time competing, I knew what I did and did not want to repeat. The attempts prior were full of self-doubt and overanalyzing the competition. Even though I had done well and placed in the top 10 two of the three times, I had never performed at my best, almost as though I was afraid to go all in.

This time I wanted nothing more than to make myself proud and hopefully earn an opportunity to start over in life. I had invested significantly in my preparation this time. I hired coaches. I practiced daily, and I was clear on why I was the best girl for the job.

Winning Miss Florida would absolutely change my life. It was a full-time job and would open more doors than I could imagine. It also came with a hefty scholarship that could help me pay for law school. Plus, it had been my *dream* since I was a child to compete on the Miss America stage. I checked in, got organized, and was grateful to be there competing for my dream job.

That week was one for the history books. Eleven of us got food poisoning during an appearance on the 4th of July, myself being one of them, and were hospitalized due to the severity. The story was all over the news as we all lay in the hallways on stretchers due to not enough bed capacity at South Miami hospital. I seriously thought my chances of even being able to compete were completely over, let alone being able to advance to the top 10.

Despite years of being a competitive athlete and working with amazing coaches to help keep my mindset in check, it wasn't translating when I was competing on these types of stages. I would self-destruct or completely wreck my mindset comparing myself to the competition. Feelings of not being good enough would surface and the inner critic inside my head would affect how I showed up. During my preparations for the 2006 competition, however, I dusted myself off, internalized the lessons I had learned, surrounded myself with support, and put myself to the test by continuing to step outside of my comfort zone. Dozens of mock interviews and practice sessions enhanced my confidence to know that I could handle whatever was thrown my way.

It turned out that getting food poisoning was one of the best things that could have happened to me. I literally didn't have the energy to think about anyone else or talk myself out of believing that I was capable of doing what I needed to do to win. I had to put my blinders on and keep my mindset strong just to have enough energy to compete. After a day in the hospital and another full day sleeping in the hotel while the remainder of the contestants went on appearances and autograph signings around town, I was beginning to regain my strength and my ability to compete was looking like a realistic possibility.

They changed the order of competition to account for those who were sick for the preliminary competitions. During preliminaries, each contestant competes in every phase of the competition, which ultimately leads to the judge's scores determining the top 10 finalists for finals night. There were 40 girls competing that week so 20 competed in prelims on Wednesday and the second group, which I was in, did prelims on Thursday, with all 40 competing in an interview competition on Friday before announcing the top 10 on Saturday night.

By the time I came out of my food poisoning fog, it was time to watch group 1 compete. My biggest competitor swept her prelim group on Wednesday night, winning every category. From that moment on, the entire vibe changed. Girls were self-destructing and checking out mentally from the competition, thinking the crown was hers.

Somehow, I still thought there was a chance.

Thursday morning came and I could barely get through rehearsals. I had to change my baton twirling talent routine because flipping upside down or spinning too much made me dizzy. Last-minute changes to routines are never ideal, but in this case, it was absolutely necessary if I wanted to be able to perform. I'll never forget the director saying, "if you can't make it through rehearsals you can't go on stage tonight. It's not safe and we won't take on that liability."

I sipped my Gatorade and tried to get some additional saltines in me. I was not going down this way. The last thing I wanted to do was pack up my stuff and go back to my apartment with my ex-fiancé.

Somehow, by the grace of God, I was able to prove to them during rehearsals that I was well enough to perform and get through all phases of the competition. I continued to pray that it was true because the nausea was raging and I still felt awful. But, after all, you miss 100% of the shots you don't take, and if I didn't make it on stage in this phase, I'd be eliminated entirely from the competition.

I managed to compete in prelims on Thursday night but I didn't win *any* of the categories. I'd be lying if I said I wasn't devastated. At that point I had two choices, stay focused or give up.

I was committed to seeing this through.

As we got closer to finals night, I was overanalyzing *everything*. The nerves that weren't there as I was trying to just keep myself from being ill during prelims had all shown up, almost as if they were making up for the lost time. On top of all of this, it was my 23rd birthday. A lot of unknowns were swirling in my head and causing me to overthink everything. I knew I had to reset my mindset or I might as well pack my bags and go home.

Thank goodness that in addition to all of the physical preparation, I had the tools in my mindset toolbox that I needed as well. I sat in a corner backstage and put in my headphones to listen to my favorite motivational playlist. I prayed over and over again and repeated my affirmations for what felt like a thousand times.

"I didn't come this far to only come this far," I thought to myself. This was my chance to make my dreams come true, plus provide a reset button that I desperately needed. It was my time to shine, and I knew that I had to show up for *me* over the next several hours if I truly wanted what I had worked so hard for. And I believed I could.

When it was time for the finals to start, we all filed onto the stage to await our fate. We did the opening number and the auditor handed the envelope to the hosts to announce the top 10. My fate was in the hands of five judges whom I had only ever seen or met in prelims, and I prayed that they believed enough in me to advance me to the top 10.

As each girl was called, my heart raced faster. As it got to the eighth girl and I was still standing behind the finalists, my eyes were welling up with tears. "Oh no. Oh no. Oh no. Just call Miami. Please, dear God, please, call Miami."

They called the ninth girl into the 10, and it was not me. It felt like everything was in slow motion and somewhat of an out-of-body experience.

Then finally. . . . "The last young woman competing for the title of Miss Florida is . . . . . . Allison Kreiger, Miss Miami."

I almost passed out. I'd been in the top 10 before but the emotional rollercoaster I'd been on seemed to exacerbate my emotions—plus being called last when there were so many other deserving young women still standing waiting to be called was a humbling experience.

I hustled down the stage into the 10, so grateful and thankful to have one more shot. We were then quickly whisked off stage to change and recompete in all phases of the competition. Thank God for adrenaline, Gatorade, and the incredible contestants backstage because I am not sure I would have made it through without each of them. The kindness displayed by so many of them is something I will never forget. And when it was time for me to recompete in talent, the wings of the stage were filled by them cheering me on as I twirled my heart out in my final attempt to make this dream come true. I knew if I could execute a solid performance, I would have the best shot at not eliminating myself from the chance to advance from the top 10 to the top 5, which was something I had yet to experience.

I hung onto the baton and had a "no-drop" performance. I took a huge sigh of relief and hustled to change into my evening gown before awaiting my fate.

The rest of the night flew by and I was called into the top five! I was in disbelief only due to what I had overcome that week to get to that moment, but I was also so extremely proud of myself for being resilient despite all of the unexpected challenges I had faced.

And because I had worked so hard on my mindset, at this point it was as if I was living out the visualization exercises that I had worked on prior to even checking in. I had envisioned this moment time and time again and had even allowed myself to see in my mind's eye that crown being placed on my head. It actually felt like it might actually happen, and I was ready.

It was finally time for crowning and suddenly I became incredibly calm. I was super aware of my surroundings, and for a few moments could see the members of the audience who were there to support me. They were all well aware of everything that was transpiring that week and I could feel their love and support from the audience more than ever before. My mentees and baton-twirling students were down in front. My family was in the middle. My coaches were off to the left, and up in the balcony was my ex-fiancé. It was a bizarre moment, as we all braced ourselves for what was about to happen next.

The theater was so loud as they called the fourth and third runners-up. Then the unexpected happened. The young woman who swept prelims whom I fully expected to be the next Miss Florida was called as the second runner-up.

As I stood there, hands held tight with the remaining contestant, the audience was silent. She looked at me and rubbed my arm as if she knew what was about to go down.

"Two to go...." The emcee said as the drumroll music played behind him. "The first runner-up and winner of a $6,000 scholarship is . . . Megan Clementi, Miss UCF. And your new Miss Florida is Allison Kreiger, Miss Miami."

Although there were still so many uncertainties about what my future would look like, what I did know was this: in that single moment my entire life changed, and forever I would have the honor of being Miss Florida 2006. I just earned myself a dream job with an expiration date, despite all of the craziness that had transpired and the odds that were stacked against me. I was about to have the opportunity to compete at Miss America and, most important, start an entirely new chapter in my life that enabled me to show up as a more aligned and focused version of myself.

As I took my first walk, overwhelmed, overjoyed, and grateful, I embraced and appreciated for the first time just how powerful you can be when you put your mind to something and stop being afraid of being amazing. I appreciated how my preparation showed up for me and how the blinders I had put on had helped block out the countless distractions that could have easily sidetracked me from success. As I looked out in the audience to a standing ovation I was overcome with emotion because I had truly proven to myself what I was capable of, even when it felt impossible.

Focus On Your Goals

I've carried with me so many of the lessons learned from that week and have applied them over and over again, and helped thousands of others realize and tap into them, too. When you are clear on your intention, invested in your success, and can drown out the noise, you can accomplish anything. Your ability to focus on the outcome will enhance your likelihood of achieving your dreams.

In Chapter 7 we are going to dive deep into goal setting, but this is a perfect opportunity to introduce you to several powerful concepts embedded in my FOCUS framework (Figure 3.1), which we will build on throughout this book.

In this process, *FOCUS* stands for *follow one course until successful*. First and foremost: get super clear on what you want and

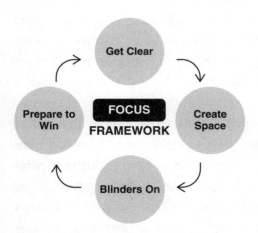

FIGURE 3.1   FOCUS framework.

commit to it. The most important thing to remember in this step is that you can only focus on one thing at a time, so you need to choose *one* single goal. The reason for this is simple: when you dilute your focus, you dilute your results. When I competed for Miss Florida 2006, my goal was to win. It became my north star and a goal I chased for a total of five years. I could have easily thrown in the towel, but I would have been throwing away the knowledge, wisdom, and experience that came with chasing that dream. Now I am not saying that quitting is never an option, but it should be reserved for when the goal you're going after is no longer in alignment with what you want, or who you want to be.

Next, create space for greatness. When you make moves that honor the version of yourself that you want to be, you'll be able to create a path that's more in alignment with your future self. Making a bold move right before I had to compete was scary, but it was also liberating. Intentionally shedding a version of myself that I didn't want to be was necessary to step into a new version. Yes, it was really hard and I would be lying if I said anything different. But it was also the weight I needed to be lifted off of me in order to truly stand in my power and show myself, and ultimately the judges, who I was and wanted to be.

Next, adopting a blinders-on mindset is critically important. If you've ever watched a horse race, you've seen the blinders that are next to the horse's eyes. This is done to prevent the horse from looking backward or getting distracted by what's around. I encourage you to think about your own blinders and what you need to drown or block out in order to stay focused on what you want for your life and career. This goes for people, too. There will always be someone who could be considered your competition, but every moment you focus or obsess on what they're doing, you're taking precious time and energy away from yourself. This was, and still is, one of the areas I focus on with my clients, and I always remind them to stop giving their energy

away to other people when they need to preserve it for themselves. Start noticing when it happens and flip the focus back to
the next thing you can do for yourself. In addition to human distractions, think about all of the things that distract you, or get in
the way of you achieving success, such as wasting time on things
that don't matter or don't help you get closer to who or what you
want to be. How can you navigate these things better or remove
them from your life or experiences? When you notice yourself
getting distracted, put your blinders on, and keep your mindset
strong. When you do so, you take back your power and help
yourself stay focused on what you need to do, rather than getting
caught up or distracted.

Last, always prepare to win. That level of preparation will
show up for you in ways you can't even imagine. The reason
I was still able to pull off winning in the story of this chapter was
that I was ridiculously prepared to compete. I went all in and that
level of commitment showed up for me even when I wasn't at my
best. And although my example had a literal crown attached to it,
it's symbolic of whatever goal, title, or level you're working to
achieve. Simply put: *do the work*. It will pay off. Plus, you become
stronger, more resilient, and more confident every step of the
way. We will talk about this a lot throughout the book but
I wanted to introduce the concept early because it pertains to
countless areas of life. Whether you're going after a new job or
position, launching a company, or simply tackling the next goal
on your list, go all in. It's far better
to invest fully in whatever it is that
you're working on rather than holding yourself back and creating built-
in excuses. You can't fully evaluate
and audit your results if you haven't
fully focused your time, energy, and
resources on them. And remember,

> *It's far better to invest fully in whatever it is that you're working on rather than holding yourself back and creating built-in excuses.*

don't be afraid of failure. The only time you truly fail is if you don't learn along the way and apply those priceless lessons and perspectives the next time.

Now let's take these concepts and get your wheels turning. Take time to think about these questions:

- Is there a current goal or opportunity that you would like to pursue?

- Have you attempted it before?
  - If so, what was the outcome?
  - If not, why?

- Is it something you're ready to pursue now?
  - Do you have the time, energy, resources, and/or support to get started?
  - If not, what do you need to do to make time?

- Are you in alignment with this next level?

- Is there anything currently standing in your way from making this goal a reality?

- What blinders do you need to put on in order for you to focus?

- Do you need to make any changes or adjustments to enable yourself to fully show up for yourself?

- What would accomplishing this mean for your future self?

This is by no means an exhaustive list, and trust me when I tell you we are going to dive deep throughout this book. I am going to ask you constantly to reflect and evaluate different areas of your life. After all, this book was created to help *you* optimize your powerful potential and that's not going to happen simply by reading it. You've got to commit to doing the work, and it all starts with creating the clarity you need to evaluate where you are versus where you want to be. Be mindful that this may stir up emotions and even potential resentment if it's something you've put off over the years. Instead of allowing yourself to feel any discontent, honor the fact that you're willing to do something about it now and give yourself grace as you begin to make moves into unfamiliar next levels and opportunities.

And, most important, if your growth requires you to make big, bold decisions in order to truly pursue who and what you want to become, trust yourself and your intuition. Deep down inside you know what you need to do, and if you take nothing else away from this chapter, please hold on to this:

> Give yourself permission to evolve into the complete person you're intended to be. Do not shrink to fit in a past version of yourself when you were born to shine. If you know you're meant for more, give yourself every opportunity to succeed. You **deserve** the time and space to work on your goals and dreams because they were placed in your heart for a reason.

Shine Bright

Master Your Mindset

Confidence Is Your Key to Success

There's a direct correlation between confidence and success, yet so many people struggle to feel good enough to truly go after what they want in their lives and careers.[1] I've always appreciated Henry Ford's quote that "whether you think you can, or you think you can't—you're right" because it encapsulates how powerful our own mindset is when it comes to accomplishing our goals. A lack of confidence affects individuals of all ages, yet there isn't an intentional focus during our formative years to build a strong foundation that enhances our self-belief and confidence in our abilities throughout our lives. Even worse, as we age, we often allow external influences to dictate our worth and how we show up—leading to reduced confidence.

---

[1]National Research Council. (1994). Self-confidence and performance. *Learning, remembering, believing: Enhancing human performance*. The National Academies Press. https://doi.org/10.17226/2303

And while some people are naturally more confident than others, there's consistent evidence that confidence and self-efficacy, an individual's belief in their capacity to execute behaviors necessary to produce specific performance attainments,[2] can be acquired using intentional, internal mindset management and making a commitment to build it. I've spent a considerable amount of time coaching and training individuals of all ages and skill levels on how to master their mindset so that they can maximize their results. It's one of the critical components of being able to show up with confidence and not take yourself out of the game along the way.

I've found great success using what I like to call the *confidence continuum* (Figure 4.1). The confidence continuum focuses on identifying what's holding you back, removing the barriers or influences that are limiting your ability, developing the skills to aid in your ability to continue to evolve, and reclaiming your internal power so that you can show up and shine bright.

Confidence can be accumulated in a variety of ways. Skill mastery and expertise yield confidence by giving you the ability to show up and make things happen. Consistent progress and proving to yourself that you are capable of doing the next right thing builds confidence. Being accepted within your social circle

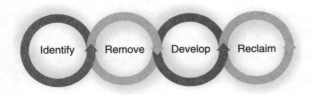

FIGURE 4.1 The confidence continuum.

---

[2]Bandura, A. (1977). Self-efficacy: Toward a unifying theory of behavioral change. *Psychological Review, 84*(2), 191–215.

or among your colleagues builds confidence. Recognition and validation of quality work or an achievement build confidence. But what happens when over time, your confidence is diminished or affected as a result of life's circumstances or experiences?

There are a whole host of challenges that can affect your confidence and mindset: perfectionism, your inner critic, fear of failure, imposter syndrome, doubt, comparing yourself to others, and many more. Any and all of these can get in the way of you showing up with confidence and owning the room.

Cultivating Confidence: My Story

I wish I could say I was a naturally confident person, but that's definitely not the case. I've been through so many seasons of doubt and insecurity that emerged for a variety of reasons, some self-inflicted and some triggered by others. All of them ultimately affected how I was showing up.

Before sharing the following story, I want to clarify that I am forever grateful to the Miss America Organization and will always love it. It literally changed my life and I'm obsessed with what this program does for young women. That is one of the many reasons I am still involved to this day. It just so happens that one of my most important life lessons happened during my time as a contestant, and I truly believe that it is relevant for anyone who is in a position to be judged or open to criticism. Especially in a day and age when social media and online forums can easily skew negative, online bullying is pervasive, and other people share their opinions often without an invitation, I want to pause and raise awareness that it doesn't matter what your profession is, what your dreams are, or who you want to be, you have to do the work to cultivate your confidence because it will be tested at some point and you don't want to have the same outcome I had.

One of the most pivotal experiences in my twenties was within hours of winning Miss Florida. The haters showed up big time and I allowed them to rock my confidence despite the huge achievement that I had just accomplished. In pageant land, there are anonymous message boards where people tear others down. They are brutal. I am not sure why I checked the boards after winning—I knew better—but something in me was searching for additional validation that I should be the new Miss Florida.

Talk about stealing my joy. They were absolutely *filled* with negativity, saying I shouldn't have won and that the judges made a huge mistake. And although I knew that I shouldn't internalize this criticism, it was pretty hard not to. I totally don't believe the old "sticks and stones" saying because oftentimes words hurt more than anything. I realize that I signed up to compete, but I didn't sign up for a brutal lashing online. Immediately, I felt like I didn't deserve any of it—from the online negativity to the Miss Florida title. Seeing those messages was upsetting, but—even worse—it triggered my imposter syndrome, and I felt like I was way out of my league.

My fragile 23-year-old self was really struggling to get those comments out of my head. Looking back, I know they weren't true, but in the moment, it was so painful. I had worked hard and prepped my heart out. It was the fourth time I had competed for the title, so I knew how to compete and what was required to win.

That was the day that laid the groundwork for a very important lesson, one that I wish I had used as a guiding light through the rest of that year, and for years after. But it took me a while to fully recognize the truth revealed by that experience: *seeking validation from others gives your power away, dims your light, and steals your joy.*

If I could turn back time, I wouldn't let myself care. I wish I had openly talked about what I was feeling, instead of letting the shame keep me silent. I was embarrassed that I had checked the boards in the first place, and I was humiliated by what I saw there and how it made me feel.

I also wished I had addressed the rest of my year as Miss Florida with the strong mindset that I had entered into it with. But as each day passed, I let others' opinions rule my year and allowed my confidence to deteriorate. Everything from what I wore, to how I looked, to what I said was influenced by others. I noticed that the longer I wore the crown, the more I sought validation from others, and the more important that became to my own self-worth. The irony is that this is the complete opposite of the mission of the Miss America Organization, which is to prepare great women for the world, and prepare the world for great women. The organization is a phenomenal launching pad and changes the lives for all involved, and I wish I would have allowed myself to fully embrace the experience rather than paying so much attention to the haters and critics online.

By the time I got to the Miss America pageant in January 2007, I didn't even recognize who I was. I had given so much weight to the opinions of others that I had stopped trusting myself.

If the July version of Allison had walked into Miss America— the person who felt calm and confident on the brink of winning Miss Florida—I am confident that I would have done much better. But that's not what happened. Instead, the version of me that showed up was out of alignment with how I had dreamed I would be. Even worse, I was someone who wasn't sure she belonged in the Miss America pageant.

I achieved my dream of competing in Miss America, but I didn't meet my placement goals—and the only person to blame for that is myself. Between July, when I won Miss Florida, and January, when I competed for the title of Miss America, I had given my power away.

Every day that I questioned whether I deserved to be there, I weakened my confidence. Every time I said yes to something I wanted to say no to, I knocked myself down. Every time I sought validation from others, I didn't trust myself. Every time I allowed someone else's opinion to drive my decision, I chipped away at my strength and confidence. Slowly, I erased the woman who was brave enough to have a life-changing conversation the week before becoming Miss Florida. The woman who had played full out, despite an annihilating case of food poisoning; who had created a nonprofit organization that had helped thousands of people with eating disorders find their voice and get the help they needed; who had traveled the world winning twirling competitions since the age of five; who had dreamed a big dream and chased it for years—that woman was missing.

Overcoming Imposter Syndrome

Imposter syndrome[3] is very real and there have been countless times that I have faced it head-on—and I know I am not alone. Imposter syndrome tends to show up as you continue to evolve, level up, or step outside of your comfort zone. You may be well qualified, work hard, and have the right experience, but you have thoughts like "Who am I to be doing this?" or "I feel like a fraud." These are common indicators that your imposter syndrome is raging.

Imposter syndrome is given voice by your inner critic, the voice in your head that brings more negativity than positivity. Your inner critic needs to be checked because the only thing it

---

[3]Robinson, A. (2017, November 1). Overcoming imposter syndrome. *Psychopharmacology and Substance Abuse Newsletter*. https://www.apadivisions.org/division-28/publications/newsletters/psychopharmacology/2017/11/imposter-syndrome

will do is talk you out of what you want or place self-doubt in your mind and keep you playing small.

Here's the deal: it's totally natural to feel uncomfortable or unworthy to hold a position or take advantage of an opportunity, especially when it's new. What's not okay is letting those feelings stop you. In fact, I firmly believe that if you're not noticing pings of those imposter feelings, you might actually be holding yourself back.

No matter how loud those negative voices are, the important thing is how you manage them. I've learned that one of the best ways to overcome imposter syndrome is to forge ahead. Borrow the confidence of those who believe in you to help you get to the next point along your path. As you continue to build up your experience, credibility, and confidence, it gets easier and easier to work through it. Plus, every time you face imposter syndrome and move through it, you build your grit and resilience, which will serve you for years to come.

As I began to learn that truth, I made a promise to myself that, regardless of what the naysayers said, I was going to finish my year strong. When I got home from the Miss America pageant, I granted myself 24 hours to cry it out, be upset, and work through it. Then, it was time to get back to work. Being Miss Florida is a full-time job, meaning I could not work elsewhere or go back to school until I was done. And work was exactly what I did. It turned out to be what my soul needed, and it was a massive confidence booster as I rebuilt myself and rewrote the script for my year of service. I was so determined to create my own legacy and leave the organization better than I found it, that I poured my heart into each and every day. I traveled a total of 80,000 miles to complete more than 250 appearances, building connections with amazing people. As a result, I opened doors for myself that I still walk through today.

That commitment to service earned me a title that I was incredibly proud of by the end of my year: the busiest and most booked Miss Florida that the organization had ever had. Which, ultimately, resulted in making a huge impact and extending the reach of the organization beyond what had been done before.

Although the first half of my reign leading up to Miss America wasn't what I had envisioned, I certainly felt that I had an incredible last six months, and I left a legacy I am proud of to this day. I got to do extremely meaningful work sharing my story of eating disorder recovery with countless individuals and advocating for change in my state and our nation's capital. I traveled to dozens of schools to inspire the next generation and spoke with the media about the work I was doing. It was an honor to participate in amazing events with rooms full of celebrities, politicians, and powerhouses, and, through it all, I made great memories that still make me smile.

I will continue to be forever grateful for being Miss Florida 2006. I will also never forget the lessons I learned from the experience and will continue to preach about the importance of valuing and honoring yourself, showing up as the most vibrant version of yourself, and, most important, trusting your intuition even if you're the only one who feels that way. I literally rebuilt my confidence in a matter of months and was able to salvage the experience because I consciously changed my mindset, showed up in the service of others, focused on why I was there in the first place, and embraced this once-in-a-lifetime opportunity, instead of worrying about what other people thought and giving their opinions more weight than my own. I've since made it my mission to be a mentor, coach, and friend to every Miss Florida after me to help them navigate the beautiful experience it is to represent their state while simultaneously juggling staying true to who they are at their core as they manage the positive and negative opinions of others.

As I look back, I am thankful that I learned this lesson early on because the more that I have put myself out there over the course of my career—speaking on stages, showing up on social media and with my podcast, and even as I write this book—the more I have had to be mindful of protecting my confidence and peace, and I want to encourage you to do the same.

Always remember that you're meant to do great things, even if it makes others uncomfortable. The haters usually show up because your success triggers their feelings of jealousy and regret. That's okay. Do what you're doing, anyway. And, most important, don't let your fear and self-doubt stop you from taking an unfamiliar action. Believing in yourself is the first step to doing what you dream. Your confidence will increase the more you do the things that lead you to your next level, and you'll gain momentum as you go. Your dreams and goals were placed in your heart for a reason. Don't take yourself out of the game by allowing imposter syndrome or your inner critic to dictate your future.

Will it always be easy? No.

Will it be worth it? 1,000% *yes*.

Coaching Confidence

As I've continued to coach and be coached, it's apparent that every new level or experience outside of your comfort zone can bring feelings of doubt and insecurity. I encourage you to acknowledge why you are feeling this way rather than believe the negative narrative that's in between your ears.

As I've advanced in my career, I've really had to be intentional about what I allow in my mind. When I first started at Advanced Recovery Systems (ARS), my lack of official experience and training in sales didn't bother me, but as we grew and the pressure intensified, it was easy for me to slip back into self-doubt, fear, and imposter syndrome if I wasn't careful.

I'll never forget saying yes to ARS. It was new and exciting. It was a chance to open a treatment center in my own community to help those struggling with addiction, eating disorders, and mental health. Plus, it was the chance to really build something amazing from scratch with the goal of growing to become a multisite, multistate company. It was a game-changing career move for me, and it offered more potential than I could even wrap my head around.

I had just finished law school, received my Juris doctorate, and only had about nine months of experience in the treatment industry. And although I had spent 10 years in the nonprofit world, I had never started a sales department, much less led a sales team. I was shooting from the hip 90% of the time, figuring things out as I went and hustling nonstop to make up for time and experience. There was no one showing me the way, so I gained confidence by learning and doing.

It had been going fine, but a few months in I got a call from our director at the time. "Allison, I need you to get a deck together. We have potential investors who are going to come and tour. This is a big deal and will be a game changer for the company."

"No problem," I said. Then, I hung up and did what every well-educated person does—I turned to Google and God. I had *no* idea what he was talking about, not to mention the fact that our growth plans when I was hired didn't include an experience like this so soon. I honestly thought I had a few years to get my act together and figure things out.

I'll never forget sitting on the floor at FedEx trying to pull together this deck and thinking, "What the hell did I get myself into?"

Imposter syndrome, self-doubt, and my inner critic were raging. *"Who do you think you are?" "Why are you in this seat?" "You're not*

good enough to do this job." "You oversold yourself." "You're unqualified."
The list goes on and on. It was the first time in this role that I had
felt super over my head and I realized I had a lot of work to do if
my efforts were ever going to meet expectations—and this was literally just the beginning. We had only been open for three months!

And while I sat there feeling completely out of my league, the
reality was they saw *something* in me that gave them the confidence to hire me and give me this chance to build an epic company. Once this deck was done, I knew I had some work to do.
I'd played this game before with myself and I knew if I didn't get
my confidence in check, I would *never* be able to be in situations
that were outside of my comfort zone. I refused to live in a state
of anxiety, always worrying about if I was good enough. It was an
important lesson about the impact that mastering your mindset
can have on your day-to-day as well as your overall results.

One of the fascinating parts about working in behavioral
health for decades is that not only is it a mission-driven industry
but also I get to be surrounded by super-smart medical and clini-
cal experts who have done extensive research on neuroplasticity
and the brain. Neuroplasticity, also known as neural plasticity or
brain plasticity, is "the ability of the nervous system to change its
activity in response to intrinsic or extrinsic stimuli by reorgan-
izing its structure, functions, or connections."[4] Add in years of
my own research, studying high performers, learning from the
best, and training hundreds of sales reps and thousands of ambitious individuals through my coaching company, and I've been
able to identify the core areas that cause people to play small in
business and life and get in the way of believing what they can do.

Back in the McKenna Walsh days, during every initial consul-
tation with a client, we would complete an exercise called "Be Your

---

[4]Mateos-Aparicio, P., & Rodríguez-Moreno A. (2019). The impact of studying brain plasticity. *Front Cell Neuroscience, 13,* 66.

Own Best Friend." We'd have very candid conversations right up front about the power of our words and the impact they have on how we show up in life. I've included that exercise for you at www .shebelievedbook.com/resources, and I encourage you to share it with your inner circle. It's a powerful reminder that we have to show up for ourselves and be kind to our minds. Ultimately, if you wouldn't say the words you say to yourself to your own best friend, you've got to stop saying them to yourself. Noticing it is half the battle and doing something about it will change your life.

In addition to practicing love and kindness toward yourself, it's critically important to remove the inner critics in our lives. One of my brilliant coaches, Dr. Laura Gallaher, shared extensive wisdom when it came to managing our inner critics, explaining how the inner critic voice can easily affect our confidence. "Name her to tame her," meaning to call out the inner critic in order to minimize its impact, quickly became a mantra for me whenever I started noticing that little voice creeping up or self-doubt sur-facing. It's amazing what happens when you take back control of your mindset. It's even more powerful when you couple naming it with overcoming your own objections. This particular practice has been a fan favorite because it's amazing how much power can be removed from your inner critic by simply acknowledging what it is that you're saying to yourself and making a list of all of the reasons that it isn't true. A very helpful practice for me and others has been creating a "win list" full of examples of all of the reasons you're qualified, giving yourself credit for the big and small mile-stones, and not losing sight of the progress that's been made. I've included a link to a powerful exercise at www.shebelievedbook .com/resources if you'd like to go deeper into this work.

One of the most impactful practices for myself and those I've coached, trained, and mentored over the years is a habitual prac-tice that disrupts your ability to allow the negative chatter to get in your way from believing in yourself. It's called the *I am* state-ment. Thanks to many amazing sessions with a mindset and mental coach when I was competing, I learned about the power of positive affirmations, which I like to call mindset mantras. You may already be familiar with the power of *I am* statements. I had heard of them, but it wasn't until the technique was explained to me in greater depth that I learned about the impact of affirmations and the scientific evidence that supports how beneficial it is to restoring self-confidence and self-worth.[5]

For me, it wasn't just about affirming what I wanted, it was about stopping negative chatter in its tracks. It's very simple, yet profound: you can't simultaneously say negative and positive things to yourself, so pick the positive and master your mindset.

Disrupting negative thought patterns from permeating my mindset has made a massive difference, and it can for you, too. And although identifying it is an important first step, learning how to rewrite the narrative you tell yourself makes a big difference in your ability to stay in a positive headspace. I appreciate Dr. Lisa W. Coyne's four-step process[6] to detach from our critical voices and build more joy, vitality, and connection in our lives:

1. **Pause.** When life gets overwhelming and your mind feels burdened, take time to *pause*. Bring yourself back into the present moment.

2. **Notice.** Being mindful of the thoughts you're experiencing will help you recognize if you're stuck in your thoughts or living in the present moment.

3. **Label.** Take a step back and be mindful of your thoughts. Identify them for what they are without taking them as literal

[5]Cascio, C. N., O'Donnell, M. B., Tinney, F. J., Lieberman, M. D., Taylor, S. E., Strecher, V. J., & Falk, E. B. (2015). Self-affirmation activates brain systems associated with self-related processing and reward and is reinforced by future orientation. *Social Cognitive and Affective Neuroscience*, 11(4), 621–629. doi.0.1093/scan/nsv136.
[6]McLean. (3 December 2022) Four ways to stop negative thinking. https://www.mcleanhospital.org/essential/negative-thinking

facts. Reframe how you perceive the situation, allowing your-self to take charge in order to move forward with clarity.

4. **Choose.** Once you have paused, noticed, and labeled your thoughts, you then choose your intention and how you want to move forward.

Back when I was working with my mindset coach during my teenage years, we came up with four, short, easy-to-remember statements that I literally engrained in my brain. I would say them all of the time and got used to incorporating them into my daily practice so that I could depend on them in times of pres-sure, stress, or when my confidence was waning. The consistent integration was the key, however, because if it wasn't my auto response, it wouldn't be what I thought of first when I noticed the self-doubt creeping in.

Done Is Better Than Perfect

In addition to having the ability to shift your mindset is the necessity of shedding the need to be perfect. Perfectionism can be a paralyzing experience and has the tendency to eat away at your confidence. It also has a high correlation with depression and can lead you down an unfulfilling path if you're not careful. As a recovering perfectionist I can personally attest to how liber-ating it has been to shed the fears of not being perfect. It took me a long time to shift my approach, and it even surfaced as advice on performance reviews from time to time. I knew that I had to make changes because if I didn't, my desire to be perfect would get in the way of me getting things accomplished. If I didn't get things accomplished, my confidence in my ability to do my job, scale a business, make important decisions, or even just show up as me would be affected.

We've got to stop wearing "per-fectionism" as a badge of honor and start realizing that done is *way* bet-ter than perfect. I've spent thou-sands of hours working on this with

Stop wearing "perfec-tionism" as a badge of honor.

others as well, and it's quite possibly one of the most transforma-tive experiences for those that struggle with it. It's one thing to hold ourselves to a high standard and expect excellence. It's another to get in our way and in a state of "analysis paralysis" because we are hung up on the minor details that don't make a major difference. Now please don't confuse my advice with pro-ducing subpar work products because that would be a negative reflection on you and how you represent yourself. Rather, I encourage you to continue to focus on the progress you're making as you continue to navigate projects, assignments, tasks, and goals rather than allow the anxiety of hitting submit, pub-lish, send, or post to cause you to sit on the final product instead of having closure and pride in the fact that you got it done. Con-sciously adopting a growth mindset will help you continue to focus on evolving rather than staying stuck in a fixed, or rigid, mindset. Even as I tackle new and completely foreign projects now, I give myself grace and allow myself to "make it messy" in the beginning; ask for support, feedback, and guidance when-ever possible; and know that I am learning and growing in the process. It's helped me tremendously, and rather than allowing perfectionism to affect my confidence in my ability to do what was asked of me, it's given me a newfound confidence in my abil-ity to figure things out.

It's also important to recognize that fear of what others will think often puts perfectionists in overdrive and can be the ulti-mate reason why they're struggling. Be mindful of giving your power away to the opinions of others, and focus on making the progress you need to make for yourself. It's been extremely interesting as I've worked with so many ambitious and successful people during my career. It's a fair estimate that at least 90% struggle as we get closer and closer to the finish line, even though they are 1,000% prepared and capable of showing up in a new light. My job at that point is to literally assure them that they're ready and that it's time to get it done. It makes me wonder how many beautiful projects, concepts, potential businesses, and ventures get left on the shelf because of this. If this sounds familiar and you recognize this within your own life, my hope is that you'll do what my clients have done: surround yourself with people who support and believe in you and will help get you across the finish line so you can make the impact you were intended to make.

You were born to make a major impact on this world. Do not let "stinkin' thinkin'" stop you from pursuing the next big goal or dream that you have. It doesn't have to be perfect, but you do have to commit to completion. Remember, learning and progressing is the most important part of the process, and other people's opinions shouldn't deter you from what you pursue. Plus you will build your confidence as you continue to take steps forward and learn as you go. Do not expect perfection from yourself. Expect that you will do the best you can in that situation and set the intention that you will grow from every experience that you have.

Comparison Is the Thief of Joy

It's also critically important that you not let comparison be the thief of your joy. We are all on our own journeys. We possess special and beautiful talents and strengths that enable us to contribute in meaningful and powerful ways, and your unique path is what was made for you. It's really easy to get caught up in what others are doing but all that does is distract you from you doing you, and it can have a direct negative impact on your confidence and progress. Instead of comparing yourself or, even worse, feeling bad about yourself as a result of it, honor what it is that you admire and then redirect your energy to you. I've seen time and time again that the comparison trap is rooted in fear, lack, and scarcity thinking, meaning "there's not enough success" for everyone. That couldn't be further from the truth. There's abundant success available to all of us and it's imperative to stop allowing someone else's milestones to negatively affect our perception of ourselves and our own worth. Remember, they are not your competition—they're proof that it can be done. Cheer for others as they accomplish their goals, because not only is it the right thing to do but also it channels your energy in the proper direction rather than causing a self-imposed spiral in the wrong direction. In positive psychology, there's a really powerful

> *Cheer for others as they accomplish their goals. Remember, they are not your competition— they're proof that it can be done.*

reminder in the positive emotions pillar, which states that for every one negative emotion we allow ourselves to experience, it takes three positive emotions to simply level set and get back to ground zero. The next time you notice yourself comparing and giving your joy away, make a conscious effort to redirect your energy. If for no other reason other than it's going to take three times as much effort to get you back on track and in a good headspace, commit to yourself and make a conscious effort to not get stuck in a comparison trap.

Own the Room

In addition to mastering your mindset and staying out of your own way mentally, it's important that we also address how you physically show up. We'll get into overall health and wellness later on in the book, but your body language and executive presence speak louder than any words you will say. Body posture, facial expressions, and how you present yourself affect how you feel and how others perceive you. There are incredibly impactful resources that I encourage you to watch and listen to if you haven't already.

Amy Cuddy's TED Talk is quite possibly one the greatest of all time when it comes to actionable advice that helps enhance your confidence by shifting your body positioning.[7] It quickly became a go-to explanation of how power posing (or superhero posing) can actually affect your hormonal levels and enhance your ability to handle situations that might otherwise cripple your confidence. She reinforces that when testosterone increases and cortisol decreases, individuals experience feelings of power and confidence that might not otherwise occur, especially in high-pressure situations.

Chin Up or Your Crown Slips

In addition, the way in which you carry yourself and connect with others makes a major difference in how you show up and are perceived. I highly encourage you to take stock of your posture, eye contact, facial expressions, and body language on a regularly occurring basis. Growing up, my mom was notorious for consistent reminders of "chin up, shoulders back." It used to drive me crazy, but the older I got and the more observant I became, I realized what a difference it had on how I felt and how I was received by others. Posture is a game changer and can set the tone for how someone else interacts with you. If you're

---

[7]https://www.ted.com/talks/amy_cuddy_your_body_language_may_shape_who_you_are?utm_campaign=tedspread&utm_medium=referral&utm_source=tedcomshare

engaged, sitting or standing tall, making eye contact, smiling when appropriate, and paying attention, you're sending the message that you are confident, capable, and present. If you're slouching over and are withdrawn, you immediately send a signal that you're not confident and even disengaged in the conversation or experience. That vibe can repel so many people and opportunities so be mindful of what unintentional messages you may be sending. And just like it's important to bake your mindset mantras into your daily life, you've got to do the same with posture.

Before you walk into a room or log on to a Zoom meeting, try my mom's advice: "chin up, shoulders back" and add in a smile. There's literally scientific proof that the muscle that is engaged when smiling sends a signal back to the brain, stimulating our reward system, and further increasing our level of endorphins (also known as happy hormones).[8] When we smile, our brain feels happier, and thus results in more positive energy, and that energy affects those around us and how we feel about ourselves. In addition to boosting your mood and experiencing a positive neurological reaction, smiling also reduces blood pressure and lowers stress hormones, so there are health benefits to it as well.[9] The impact it has on others is also significant. Countless studies have shown that the very act of seeing another person smile triggers an automatic muscular response in the observer, meaning you're able to trigger positive emotions in someone else simply by smiling.[10] People like to be around people who make them feel good, and your ability to positively influence someone's emotions can be magnetic.

---

[8]Intermountain Health. The health benefits of smiling. https://www.sclhealth.org/blog/2019/06/the-real-health-benefits-of-smiling-and-laughing/#:~:text=When%20you%20smile%2C%20your%20brain,the%20serotonin%20is%20an%20antidepressant.

[9]APS. (2012 July 30). Grin and bear it! Smiling facilitates stress recovery. https://www.psychologicalscience.org/news/releases/smiling-facilitates-stress-recovery.html

[10]Solara Mental Health. Say cheese! The effect of smiling at others. https://solaramentalhealth.com/the-effect-of-smiling-at-others/

Dress the Part

When it comes to your attire, please focus on what is the most flattering to you and your body type versus whatever the latest trend is. Take pride in your appearance and how you present yourself. You don't have to wear expensive clothes or the latest trend to make a statement and feel great. Make sure your clothes fit well and always make sure you're comfortable both sitting and standing.

Build Your Brand

And last, I want to share with you my experience that has made the biggest difference in enhancing the confidence of those I've worked with, coached, trained, and mentored over the years, and it all comes back to doing the work and building your brand. And when I say brand, I am not talking about logos, fonts, and colors. I am talking about *you* and what you're known for. Each and every one of us has our own personal brand, but it's what you do with it that makes a difference. Taking the time to really work on your brand is a game changer for your personal and professional growth and development, but the internal benefits are beyond what I am capable of explaining through words. We're going to get into the nitty-gritty of how later in the book, but I want to plant this seed now as a powerful reminder that *you* have everything you need within you to enhance your own confidence and represent yourself to the best of your ability. Intentionally packaging your brand will not only attract amazing opportunities to you but you'll also gain confidence as a result of doing the work.

One of the things that I absolutely *love* about helping people build their brands is witnessing the internal transformation that takes place as confidence is gained during the brand-building process. When they actually take stock of how incredible they are and we shine a spotlight on it, they become more confident. As we work to really package their brand and tell their story, their confidence is elevated as they take ownership and pride in who they are. It's literally one of the most incredible things to experience as a coach and why I continue to do the work that I do. The transformation that transpires changes them *forever* and they start to see themselves in a whole new light. When that happens, their confidence propels them forward and they're willing to take brave and bold risks because they know who they are at their core and what they're capable of. Ultimately, and most important, their level of happiness increases, and they're able to own who they are and enjoy the experiences in front of them knowing that they are fully capable of tackling whatever is next. And if at any time their confidence is dwindling, they've got me in their corner ready to build them up and remind them that they can do anything they set their mind to.

My intention for this chapter is to open your eyes to the power of confidence and hopefully encourage you to focus your energy and effort on yours. Consciously and consistently working on your confidence will continue to benefit you. And, yes, so much about confidence is really about mastering your mindset and doing a checkup from the neck up to ensure those common barriers like fear, imposter syndrome, perfectionism, and our inner critics aren't becoming permanent blockers to our own success. I want to empower you to consciously take action and do the things you need to do to elevate your confidence at every opportunity. Just like any habit, with repetition, it will become an auto-response and reaction. It will become easier, and even enjoyable, over time, and you'll be blown away by what investing in your confidence will do for your future. You're worth it and please know that you're already "enough." Now it's about raising your awareness and consciousness about what else you're capable of when you truly show up, believe in yourself, and build your brand.

Remember, I believe in you 1,000%, and my goal is that you do, too.

A Checkup from the Neck Up

Take Care of Yourself

"Are you going to get out of bed?" my husband said as he peered into our bedroom. It was 6 p.m. and I wanted nothing to do with celebrating the new year. I had no words, just tears. I rolled over, buried my face in the pillow, and sobbed.

Why am I feeling this way? I have no right when so many people are going through way worse things than we are, I thought to myself. This had been a common narrative for months, as I attempted to shove down my feelings and hide from my truth. The exhaustion, fatigue, stress, insomnia, and irritability were overwhelming. The occasional chest pains and prickly cheeks from my raging anxiety were becoming way too normal.

This particular New Year's Eve I was on an emotional precipice. The thought of a new year filled with new opportunities and goals is something I typically look forward to. However, on December 31, 2020, I laid in bed sobbing, with my chest aching, extremely exhausted at the thought of another day, let alone another year filled with unknowns and uncertainty. I vividly remember trying to minimize my negative feelings by comparing my life to others. That was the wrong thing to do. Despite working in behavioral health, I had stared straight at my own burnout journey and had done nothing to help myself. I had allowed my work addiction to become how I numbed out in an effort to convince myself that everything was going to be alright.

I had lost sight of the reality that mental health is health and that if I wasn't making time for wellness, I would be making time for illness.

Leading a national team through a devastating time filled with so many uncertainties, feeling as though the rug was being ripped out from underneath us, and going through our own personal challenges at home, was more than I could bear. Sadly, this wasn't my first experience with burnout, but this time looked and felt different than before, so I didn't immediately recognize what was going on.

It got to the point where I could barely function and I came very close to walking away from everything I had worked so hard to create at ARS. In my own business, I was able to restructure what I was doing and regain joy from the clients and projects that I was involved in. I also audited all of the other areas of my life that I was giving my time and energy and "unsubscribed" from unnecessary obligations for the sake of self-preservation. But there was still another mountain to climb at Advanced Recovery Systems (ARS).

One of the hardest parts was being vulnerable at work. I was foolish to think that others didn't see I was deteriorating, even though I tried to show up each day with a smile on my face. I realize now that so many of my challenges stemmed from my own ego and not wanting to admit weakness. I was also terribly concerned that any slip in performance would have a compounding impact on the organization and I would be replaced. I also didn't want others to see me struggle because I knew how much they depended on my optimism to help keep them in a good mindset and positive about the future state of the organization.

Ultimately, fear of what would happen kept me silent for way too long.

I wasn't just experiencing burnout from the overwhelming number of responsibilities on my plate, I was also woken up to the reality that I no longer wanted to hustle the way I once did. Signing up for excessive travel was not what I wanted. The pandemic opened my eyes to the enormous amount of life that I had missed out on. Even when I wasn't traveling the country, the long days would have me rolling in shortly before bedtime, and I was missing out on precious moments that I could never get back.

I did not want that to be the story any longer, and the thought of returning to that life was paralyzing.

As the days and months passed, I returned to therapy, sought medical treatment for the chest pains, and worked with Dr. Laura Gallaher, an amazing organizational psychologist and leadership coach. And although I did a lot of work in how I managed and navigated stress, the root of the problem still had not been properly addressed. I knew the only way to truly make things better was to address the situation head-on.

I'll never forget the day I was sitting in the boardroom with my boss. We were talking about all of the organization's upcoming needs that were going to have me zig-zagging across the country. I was needed in Ohio and New Jersey. I needed to clear space to work on a new strategy for one of the divisions within the organization, and I needed to speed up by hiring twice as many sales reps while overhauling our training and development program.

I must have turned completely pale, and for someone who loves spray tans, that's saying a lot. My boss looked at me and said, "Are you ready for this?"

I had no words as I fought back tears. I let out a huge sigh, and thankfully that sigh spoke for me.

He knew things needed to change, and I finally admitted they needed to as well. For the first time in a long time, I was completely honest about how I was feeling. I was carrying too big a load, and we both knew it. He was willing to restructure the department and carve out areas for me that were much more aligned with my desires.

Over the next several weeks and months, we transitioned many of my team members to new supervisors, delineated responsibilities, and allowed the dust to settle. I gave up a huge part of my work identity, which was a challenging experience for my ego and pride, but I was extremely proud to be a champion for my own well-being and encourage others to do the same.

Although the pivot at work was an important piece of the puzzle, I still had more internal work to do. Thankfully, my amazing support team who helped me heal and prepare for that conversation was there to support me, and I added to that team to ensure that I could do what I needed to do to prioritize my own needs so I could continue to take care of others. Day by day, I reclaimed my life and learned how to integrate small changes to have a major impact on how I felt and how I was honoring all the things that were important to me.

When I had time to take a step back and evaluate the situation, it became crystal clear that I had been focusing on what was wrong for more than 20 years, as our treatment centers were there to help people on their worst days. Working in the behavioral health industry for two decades can wear on you if you're not taking care of yourself. Hard calls, deeply emotional stories, and in some cases, tragic endings add up. Add leading through a pandemic, and it was no wonder I was depleted. But even if that weren't the case, it became evident that naturally we, as a society, tend to lean on the negative, or what needs to be fixed, rather than focusing on what's right and amplifying it.

It's commonly known that how you take care of yourself has a dramatic impact on your ability to accomplish the things you want to accomplish or simply live a healthy life. The correlation among nutrition, sleep, restoration, and exercise has a profound impact on your quality of life. The more intentional you can be about these four areas, the higher the likelihood of disease prevention and overall health and well-being. That, coupled with stress management, can change your trajectory and increase your life span.

It's also important to acknowledge that there is a direct connection between how you take care of yourself and the quality of your mental and physical health. You must regularly check in with yourself to ensure that you are not experiencing unusual symptoms that could be cause for concern. I've seen over the years that it is often a slow decline that isn't necessarily immediately recognizable, which can often be more challenging to detect.

Over the years, the glorification of hustle culture has perpetuated a way of life that's not sustainable, ultimately deteriorating the quality of our lives. And although stress is a natural response that came about during our primitive existence as a way to protect us from harm (i.e., the lions, tigers, and bears), I've noticed that far too many of us invite high levels of stress into our lives, knowingly and unknowingly.

The pandemic turned the world upside down with increased daily stressors alongside a lack of work-life balance. A study in 2022 by Zippia found that 86% of employees who work from home full-time experience burnout, while 51% of remote workers feel they don't have support from their employer to deal with issues related to being burnt out.[1] Efforts are underway in an attempt to make things right again, but it's clear not everyone is feeling relief.

What we've experienced as a global community is not something that can be easily dismissed. The pandemic was a traumatic experience, and recovering from it is an inside job, meaning we need to process the experience, get support if needed, and allow ourselves the time and space to heal. If you haven't taken the time to really reflect and assess how you're doing mentally and emotionally, you need to. The escalation of our emotions and stress response to it is a necessary discussion that we need to have.

Stress takes a toll on your emotional and mental well-being, which has physical consequences as well. Chronic stress negatively affects your heart, your ability to fight off illnesses, and your gut health, to name a few health consequences.[2]

When your gut health is affected, you can't absorb nutrients or break down the food you consume, two mechanisms that are necessary for vitality. When you are stressed, your cortisol and adrenaline hormones shift into survival mode, which limits your body's natural ability to maintain gut health and will result in fatigue, brain fog, irritable bowel syndrome, and more. It's even more important when you think of it through the lens of disease prevention. It's known that 80% of the immune system is housed in the gut wall lining,[3] and when that's affected, your immune

[1]Zippia. (2022, September 19). 35+ compelling workplace collaboration statistics [2022]: The importance of teamwork. Zippia.com., https://www.zippia.com/advice/workplace-collaboration-statistics/

[2]American Psychological Association. (2018, November 1). Stress effects on the body. https://www.apa.org/topics/stress/body

[3]Wiertsema, S. P., van Bergenhenegouwen, J., Garssen, J., & Knippels, L. M. J. (2021). The interplay between the gut microbiome and the immune system in the context of infectious diseases throughout life and the role of nutrition in optimizing treatment strategies. *Nutrients*, *13*(3), 886. doi:10.3390/nu13030886

system is much more likely to be compromised, which limits your body's ability to aid in disease prevention.

Additionally, over 90% of serotonin, your "happy hormone," is housed in the gut.[4] When you experience lower levels of serotonin, it increases your risk of depression, anxiety, and sadness. Because stress typically affects your cortisol level, your cognitive function may also be impaired.[5] It can also have a negative impact on the female reproductive cycle, leading to negative outcomes when trying to conceive a child or carry a pregnancy to term.[6]

As I'm sure you've picked up on, this is an area that I am begging you to address. Auditing your stress levels and making shifts to better manage them will affect your quality of life in substantial ways. Noticing when you are experiencing greater levels of stress at the moment and connecting them back to what you were doing or experiencing is a great first step. I also highly encourage you to keep a log for at least two weeks so you can identify trends and be more mindful of what triggers you. And although I wish we could remove all stress from our lives, the solution isn't to wish it away, but rather to remove what you can and learn how to better manage stressful situations and people.

Breathwork, meditation, mindfulness, yoga, therapy, and support groups are just a few suggestions that have helped me and many others over the years. I've included an extensive list of resources on www.shebelievedbook.com/resources if this is an area that you need more help with on your journey. I'm a work in progress, too, so please come as you are and try new things. I always say that it's important to have multiple tools in your

---

[4]Terry, N., & Margolis, K. G. (2017). Serotonergic mechanisms regulating the GI tract: Experimental evidence and therapeutic relevance. *Handbook of Experimental Pharmacology, 239*, 319–342. doi:10.1007/164_2016_103

[5]de Souza-Talarico, J. N., Marin, M. F., Sindi, S., & Lupien, S. J. (2011). Effects of stress hormones on the brain and cognition: Evidence from normal to pathological aging. *Dementia & Neuropsychology, 5*(1), 8–16. doi:10.1590/S1980-57642011DN05010003

[6]https://www.webmd.com/baby/features/infertility-stress

toolbox and that acknowledging it is half the battle. You should not live life in a perpetual state of stress because it's the fastest way to shorten your time here on earth and impair the quality of the time that you have.

Health = Wealth

The sixth pillar in positive psychology and the shining star of this chapter is the health pillar. I'll share with you the four core areas that have a profound impact on your ability to show up as the version of yourself that you dream of. Even a slight deterioration within the health quadrant can lead to a declining mental and physical state. Most important, I urge you to treat your mental health just as seriously as you do your physical health. If you get sick, chances are you're calling your doctor, logging on to Teladoc, or going to urgent care. My hope is that when you start to notice changes in your mental health you take the same approach. I highly encourage seeking out mental health support virtually or in person when you notice yourself not feeling "normal." I've included a list of resources at www.shebelievedbook.com/resources. A checkup from the neck up can change your life. It's critically important to honor what you've been through, what you're going through, and how you want to show up in the future. There is no shame in asking for help, surrounding yourself with support, and honoring your mental wellness. After all, mental health is health.

If it doesn't bring you peace, purpose, or profits, don't give it your time, energy, or attention.

Let's start with an assessment of what's really going on in your life. I've noticed over the years that it's not until I pause and make a list of all of my intentional, or sometimes even unintentional, responsibilities and commitments that I realize how overextended I've allowed myself to become. In recent years, I've embraced a concept to help me decide what to keep and what to set aside. If it doesn't bring you peace, purpose, or profits, don't give it your time, energy, or attention. Now we need to take it a few steps further.

How many responsibilities are you carrying? Saying yes can be fun, exciting, and exhilarating, but waking up with feelings of overwhelm or depleted joy is not the goal.

You can't be amazing if you're exhausted, out of alignment with your goals, or spreading yourself too thin. As you continue to elevate your career, it's critically important to prioritize and pulse-check regularly to ensure you are optimizing your potential without sacrificing your well-being and wasting your energy.

It's time to ruthlessly audit your life and where you are spending your time. If something isn't bringing you joy, you have the ability to make the changes necessary to rewrite the story. *But it all starts with you.* I know it can be scary, but your life was meant to be *extraordinary*. If you're doing too much, or not doing the things that light you up from the inside, you owe it to yourself to change.

Oftentimes, the best solution is to cut back so you can lean in. I use the analogy of pruning a rose bush. Cutting it back enables it to bloom beautifully; otherwise, its beauty is diminished and it doesn't thrive. Doing too many things at once only dilutes your focus, which in turn dilutes results.

In addition to my battle with burnout, there have been multiple, significant times in my life and career when I've had to give something up or step back from a role, and I am so much better for it despite the feelings that surfaced during the experience.

When I first started at ARS, I was doing it all when it came to marketing, business development, and branding for the organization. I ran point on liaising with our agency partners, starting our business development team from scratch, creating all of our marketing materials, speaking on behalf of the organization across the country, plus a million other random things that came from being employee number two. As a single location small start-up at the time, this was doable. But as we grew, and the needs of the organization grew, things had to change. I would be lying if I said this was easy. I had so much pride in what I had created thus far, but I didn't know what I didn't know. When ARS decided it was time to fully bring digital marketing in-house rather than work with outside agencies, we had to hire a digital savant. Part of me was crushed, but I also knew it was in the best interest of the company. Fast forward to today, and I've shed many other roles as I have continued to evolve, and the organization's need for expertise increased. A mindset shift that helped tremendously was that just because I can do something, doesn't mean I should. There are really talented people out there who can and should be focusing on what they do best. I encourage you to look at that fact as a good thing, rather than a bad thing, and delegate or delete anything that doesn't need to be on your plate (more to come on this later when we get into time management and goals). It's also a liberating experience when you can let go of the parts of your ego that are holding you back so you can flourish and focus.

Saying yes when it comes to supporting causes that I care about has been a consistent theme in my life, but it's also been my Achilles' heel. This started at an early age. My mom even gifted me a coffee mug while I was in college (that I still have, by the way) that boldly states "Note to self: Stop volunteering for stuff." And although, yes, so many of those activities gave me joy and filled up my heart, there were many occasions where once again I stayed the course way too long. In some cases, I served on nonprofit boards for over five years each, which isn't necessarily a good thing. While it's wonderful to give back, if you're over-committing yourself and sacrificing your ability to take care of yourself because you're so busy taking care of everything and everyone else, eventually there will be nothing left to give. Remember that every time you say yes to something or someone, you're potentially saying no to yourself.

For many people, myself included, people pleasing coupled with a scarcity mindset can cloud our judgment. But here's the truth: your sanity is way more important than what someone else thinks of you. Plus, there will always be other opportunities for you to contribute your time, energy, and talents.

It's far more effective to pare down what's on your list to enable you to fully show up and shine bright, rather than say yes to everything and feel completely out of control. I get it. I am a multi-passionate, say-yes kind of person, too, and I know that FOMO (fear of missing out) is real, especially as you chase career and life goals, but I promise you, you will maximize the experience so much more if you're doing *less* at one time.

Last, I want to mention something that I didn't experience until I became a mother. That's right, fellow parents, it's parental guilt. I know it's

You can't be amazing if you're exhausted.

hard to prioritize yourself once you've laid eyes on your precious tiny human, but you have to. Make a commitment to yourself now to preplan and *schedule* the time you need for yourself—and *do not* cancel on yourself. Your kids need you to be happy, and I promise you that your fuse won't be as short, you won't be as exhausted, and you will have a better quality of life if you take care of yourself, first. It's not selfish; it's self-care.

I encourage you to think about what roles in your life or at work you can step back from, either temporarily or permanently, so you can truly flourish. Download an audit at www.shebelievedbook.com/resources to help give you perspective.

Boundaries Are Beautiful

Ahhh, the good ole *B* word. My relationship with boundary setting has been an interesting one, and it would be a tremendous missed opportunity if we didn't discuss how life-changing this skill can be.

In the early days of my career, I said yes to pretty much anything and everything. I answered phone calls at all hours of the day and night, and out of fear of disappointing others, I sacrificed myself. Chalk this up to another lesson learned the hard way, but it's something that I have now gained much more control over as I've narrowed my focus and learned how to prioritize what really matters in my life and career.

Here's the truth: setting boundaries is one of the greatest acts of self-respect. They are important in both business and in life. Setting boundaries and establishing what you will or will not tolerate is how you teach people how to treat you. Never forget that access to you is a privilege, so protect your time, energy, and attention like the gold that it is.

I realize that this can be easier said than done, but I want you to know that it's absolutely possible. But first, you need to know when they're needed and what they do.

One of the best indicators is how you naturally respond to people or situations. If you are feeling anxious, resentful, offended, dreadful, or just plain don't want to do something, evaluate if creating a boundary would be helpful. For example, after the complete blur of when I was or was not available to take calls, and it came time to be at home with my kids, I set the new boundary that I would not answer the phone after 6 p.m. unless it was an emergency. My family deserves my attention and focus, and I need to restore myself in order to be able to show up the next day with the fire to tackle new challenges. Before I set this boundary, by Wednesday I was depleted, and I was less productive and miserable. That had a direct impact on my quality of work, how I treated others, and my overall well-being. Putting that boundary in place has been a game changer and has also given me the confidence to do it in other ways, too.

I had to teach people how to treat me, and I had to stick to it for my sanity and my family's. A few simple techniques helped me stick to this boundary: no phones at the dinner table and keeping my phone on silent were two that were very helpful. It was a simple shift with a significant result, and I've continued to put boundaries in place ever since.

What boundaries should you or could you set to enhance your quality of life?

The Four Points of Your Crown

By now it's clear that I am a huge fan of crowns, but I thought it would be fun to give you a visual representation to help memorize the four components of the health quadrant in positive psychology that contribute to your mental and physical well-being:

- Nutrition
- Movement
- Sleep
- Restoration

As you think about your crown in the context of your own health and well-being, consider what responsibilities you wear on a daily basis and use these four points to conduct your own self-care audit. In order to fully show up as the vibrant individual that you are—before you can undertake your commitments and your self-care—you must put your crown on first. Why? To give yourself an important reminder: you matter and you must take care of yourself each and every day.

As you think about your crown, I'd love for you to think about it from the perspective of health and total wellness, meaning that the four points represent what you need to do for yourself to be your best. The health quadrant in positive psychology reminds us that it's not just about the common three areas we all recognize—sleep, nutrition, and exercise—but it also highlights the need for intentional restoration throughout the day. I've included a copy of the health quadrant assessment at www.shebelievedbook.com/resources to help you identify where you are currently and what area(s) may need attention. Regardless, all four are critically important to your mental and physical wellness. Using the quadrant in Figure 5.1, rate yourself on a scale of 1–10, with

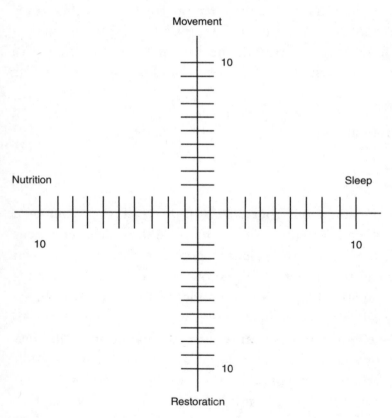

FIGURE 5.1   The four components of the health quadrant.

1 needing a lot of attention and 10 being managed extremely well. This will help you identify where you need to improve and enable you to set goals for each of these four areas if needed.

When I was going through my positive psychology coach certification program,[7] I remember initially not giving as much weight to the importance of each and its impact on how I was showing up. Although I was doing a good job with nutrition and a moderately good job with movement and exercise, I had been dismissive of my own sleep hygiene and I was not baking in any restorative breaks or practices in my day. When I made a game plan and started implementing changes like going to bed earlier, not falling asleep in my kid's rooms during bedtime (I'm known for snuggles turning into sleep sessions), and intentionally having restoration breaks throughout the day, whether it was walking outside for 5–10 minutes, using a grounding mat, or incorporating movement and music, it made a massive impact on my ability to maintain energy and be more efficient with my time. Instead of grinding through, I was able to break it up and get more accomplished in less time. I also wasn't nearly as tired at the end of the day and could be more attentive and focused, which definitely affected the quality of my work and personal interactions. It was an important reminder that *when you're tired, you need to learn to rest, not quit. Everyone needs to recharge.*

There's a direct link among the four areas of the health quadrant, your energy levels, and your ability to show up and slay like you are meant to. So please take ownership of your crown. Be honest with where you are in your health journey and make the adjustments to maximize how you show up every day. Although we can't prevent every illness or health challenge, we can take ownership of what we do and how we manage our wellness routine.

---

[7]https://www.positivepsychologycoachacademy.com/

Never forget, that you are *worth* it. The time you spend investing in your own health and well-being will make a massive difference in the quality of your life. Do what you need to do for *you*. Seek professional guidance, support, and assistance as needed and take a proactive, preventive approach rather than reactive. I promise, your future self is thanking you already.

6

Relationships Matter
It Takes a Village

The quality of your relationships will have a significant impact on the quality of your life. In fact, a review of over 400 scientific studies was published in the *Personality and Social Psychology Review* highlighting the fact that strong relationships are a vital prerequisite to being a thriving, successful human being.[1]

It's amazing how the company we keep affects us personally and professionally, yet so many of us struggle with the open-door policy we have created for ourselves when it comes to letting in too many people who don't align with our values, goals, and true selves. This tends to be an easier way to exist compared to seeking out people who will challenge and change us in all of the best ways, but it's a decision that forces us outside our comfort zones

[1]Feeney, B. C., & Collins, N. L. (2015). A new look at social support: A theoretical perspective on thriving through relationships. *Personality and Social Psychology Review*, *19*(2), 113–147. https://doi.org/10.1177/1088868314544222

and familiar social circles and unlocks possibilities that you aren't even aware of yet.

Consider this statement, so poignantly made by legendary self-help guru and motivational speaker Jim Rohn: "You are the average of the five people you spend the most time with."[2] This can serve as a wake-up call when it comes to discussing our relationships and their influence on our lives. Hearing that quote opened my eyes to those I was surrounding myself with and required me to look inward and really decide if their involvement in my life was in my best interest moving forward. I made massive decisions to consciously remove negative and toxic relationships, and doing so completely changed the trajectory of my life.

You're probably familiar with the saying that "people come into your life for a reason, a season, or a lifetime," but my hope is that after reading this chapter you'll evaluate if individuals in your life are crossing categories and intentionally or unintentionally affecting how you show up in this world. Then I'll provide the opportunity for you to decide what to do next while simultaneously encouraging you to create new relationships that will add tremendous value to your life and career. Life is too short to be playing small with your potential, so if a relationship realignment is necessary in order to unlock your ability to truly blossom, my hope is that this lights the fire within you to make the moves you need to make.

As I've continued to train hundreds of sales reps, build my online community, speak on stages, and coach my clients, whenever the conversation about relationships comes up, it's met with a lot of emotion. This response is natural because so many of us place tremendous value on those around us, and their opinions. I find myself having repetitive conversations about whom we

---

[2]https://www.goodreads.com/author/quotes/657773.Jim_Rohn

allow in and what we tolerate, especially as we evolve into the people we want to be. Other people's opinions are none of your business and should serve as a reminder of the power we give away on a regular basis to other people who are *not* living our lives. The truth is this is your life, not theirs, and if you're noticing others resisting your transformation, evolution, or advancement, you need to do something about it. The vast majority of the time you don't (or at least shouldn't) owe anyone an explanation for changing.

On the flip side, genuine, authentic, enriching relationships can have the most profound ripple effect. Not only will they help you become a better person, but they will also enable you to show up and contribute significantly to the lives of others. The older I've gotten, the more vocal I have become about my preference to surround myself with individuals who are talking about chasing dreams, conquering goals, leveling up, and building their wealth and health. The conversation is very different and aligns with the version of myself that I am working to become.

We're going to get really honest with ourselves over these next few pages because it cannot be stated enough that the relationships in your life have a direct impact on the way you show up, the goals you chase, the way you feel about yourself, and so much more. Relationships form one of the pillars in positive psychology because they are quite possibly the most important things in our lives. We are going to look at your relationships with those closest to you, the professional relationships that should exist, and the ones that no longer make sense for you, at least during this phase of life. In addition to studies showing that those with deep, meaningful relationships live longer and have happier lives, we are going to get clear on the relationships you need to have that might be lacking. We're going to talk about the importance of mentorship and surrounding ourselves with people who help us elevate in all areas of our lives. Most important, the removal of toxic influences is necessary, yet it is sometimes the hardest thing to do, so we're going to spend time discussing when we need to move on from relationships that are no longer healthy or positive. As we progress, we're going to do a deep dive and social circle audit, and I'm going to share with you helpful exercises that will help you repair relationships that need it, release those that need to go, and embrace those that need to be protected and maintained. And, of course, I'll also take the opportunity to discuss and reinforce that the most important relationship here on earth is the one you have with yourself.

Quality over Quantity

Though we often think of our relationships with others in terms of quantity, it's the quality of those relationships that really matter. A few close, supportive relationships are far more valuable than a large number of surface-level connections, which can be a challenging perspective for some to embrace.

I'll never forget my mom sharing with me at an early age that I would be lucky if I had five really good friends by the time I was in my thirties. This blew my mind as, I have to admit, I was a "more is better" kind of girl early on. However, just like with most things, she was right. Although I adore the network that I have created over the years and value the amazing friendships that I have formed, I really only let a handful of people have a front-row seat at the show. The older I've gotten, the more I've realized that true friendship makes a difference and it is very much a two-way street. Developing deep, meaningful relationships takes work and, just like with everything else, has to be prioritized. I also made the conscious decision to no longer be available for superficial people or those who drain me mentally, emotionally, or physically. I have zero tolerance for negativity in my life because, as you remember from an earlier chapter, it takes three times as much energy to level set to a positive state of mind after being exposed to negativity. Because the source of negativity is usually connected to a human, distancing oneself can be a very useful strategy for protecting one's peace, in addition to learning how to manage your response and reaction to negative and toxic people when it can't be avoided.

Honoring Those in Your Inner Circle

If you have a spouse or significant other, that relationship must be of utmost importance. If kids are also in the mix, you have to work that much harder to make sure you have dedicated time with one another to not allow the relationship you have to fall by the wayside. Scheduling and prioritizing one-on-one time has to happen as you get busier, or you run the risk of neglecting the person that you've chosen as your numero uno. My husband and I have to do this, just like I have to schedule my self-care time and other priorities. We have three very busy kids and if we're not careful, way too much time passes without us working on us for us. At the time of writing this book, we have three kids under the age of 11, and their schedules are jam-packed with every-thing they love to do. He knows me well enough to know that I have to be removed from "my environment" to be able to really relax and be together, meaning away from the house, the hustle and bustle, and distraction-free. I cherish that time and appreci-ate all of the moments that we have when it's just us. We also are in tune with each other's needs and what matters most. I highly encourage you to take the love language quiz online, which I have also linked for you at www.shebelievedbook.com/resources, and share your results with those in your life who hold a special place in your inner circle. This has also been a fabulous tool even at work to know what our people need and value, but at a bare minimum, do it for the individuals who are most sacred to you. Whether it's a significant other, or best friend, knowing what they need at this level leads to a deeper connection.

Outside of romantic relationships, my relationships with friends vary greatly. I love that some of my best friends and I talk regularly, while others can go for months with no conversations, yet we'll pick up right where we left off. The most important element with all of them though is that we love, adore, respect, and honor each other, and we want nothing but the best for one another. We'd go to bat for each other and we're always cheering each other on as we navigate the messy and amazing chapters of life. They know for certain that I would mention their name in a room full of opportunities and will show up for them whenever and wherever needed, and the feeling is mutual on my end. That type of deep connection and adoration is something I never take for granted.

It wasn't always this way, though, and unfortunately, it was a lesson I learned the hard way after giving way too much power away to others. There was a time in my life when I allowed myself to be influenced by those who did not have my best interest at heart. I allowed my people-pleasing tendencies to cloud my judgment, which resulted in ending up in places and spaces that were not beneficial for who I truly wanted to be. I let far too many people in and the quality of relationships I had suffered because I didn't take care of them the way that I should have. Several were what I now consider "wolves in sheep's clothing," meaning their outward representation was not in alignment with their motives, and removing them took way longer than it should have. These types of relationships take a much greater toll on your mental and emotional well-being than you realize at the moment, especially if they're also laced with ill intent. Challenging relationships and the impact they've had has been a common topic as I have coached and mentored hundreds of amazing women over the years. They're often disappointed in themselves for giving their power away and allowing others to affect the decisions they make or the path they take because they're worried about what others will think. Auditing your social circle and the influence they have on your decisions and life is an important exercise as you continue to navigate your life and career. Always remember that this is *your* life and if someone's influence or opinions are causing you to not do the things you want to do, represent yourself the way you want to be represented, or influence you in a negative way, you should consider distancing yourself.

I also recognize and realize that some of the most challenging and difficult relationships can stem from our own family trees, but that doesn't mean that you can't protect yourself, your dreams, and your decisions from those who might not be able to be removed. Being intentional about the amount of time or influence you allow them to have makes a big difference. Politely declining invitations to gatherings or social events that could lead to toxicity, negativity, or your detriment is important. Chances are it won't be easy but you deserve to create the space you need to take care of yourself.

It's important to be mindful that although some relationships are for a lifetime, the majority probably will not be. As you evolve, your relationships should evolve, too, and although it can be hard, sometimes the best thing to do is bless and release those who are no longer in alignment with

> *Sometimes the best thing to do is bless and release those who are no longer in alignment with who you are or where you're headed.*

who you are or where you're headed. You don't owe anyone an apology for changing and it's imperative that you don't stunt your growth because of them.

I've had this conversation countless times, especially with high-achieving, driven women, who have a long list of things they want to accomplish in their lives. It's a common and recurring theme that relationships can be challenged when one of the individuals involved is committed to growth and leveling up and the other is not. It's important to recognize that it's not uncommon for relationships to be strained when you're chasing after goals that are unfamiliar or might not make sense to others. For example, I have many clients who have pursued professional paths that require a substantial and significant commitment in order to be successful. They've faced backlash from those closest to them because they're not available as much as they used to be, or could no longer attend as many social gatherings as they once did as a result of professional pursuits and obligations. Catty comments, cold shoulders, and passive-aggressive behavior have resulted and caused hurt feelings and sadness, rather than the support they really needed. It's important to remember that when we stay committed to our own growth, it may trigger jealousy or envy because the other person is not doing what they need or want to do for themselves. Other times, it's that you're changing and they subconsciously want to keep you as the version of you that they're most familiar with. Please note, if you find yourself "shrinking" to make others comfortable, we've got a problem. Again, this can be made even more difficult if the person is related to you and you can't fully detach, so we've got to learn how to handle the opinions of those who matter to us. Suggestions that have helped me over the years have been learning how to address it head-on, knowing how to redirect the conversation, and acknowledging that I hear their concerns. Statements like "I know I haven't been able to be present recently, but I would appreciate your understanding and support during this season of my life and career" can go a long way. And in other situations, refraining from having discussions about things that frankly aren't their business unless I make it so has been very helpful. Just like we discussed boundaries in Chapter 5, it's important to create them in relationships that aren't able to be beneficiaries of distance.

You teach people how to treat you by the boundaries you create and what you will tolerate, so make sure that you are crystal clear about what you will or will not accept in the relationships that exist in your life (especially those that are most challenging). This can be as simple as verbalizing and sharing with those around you what is going on and why you need time and space. Remember, clear is kind, and it's better to be transparent and honest than not. If your boundaries are not being respected by those around you, that's a lesson in and of itself. You may need to consider the role they play in your life and whether or not they should be a part of your life.

If you feel as though you've been neglecting relationships, or if you're simply looking to strengthen the relationships you currently have, consider using a tool right out of the positive psychology toolbox: the gratitude letter. You may or may not send this letter but it enables you to put your words on paper and really appreciate the amazing people you have in your life. The recipient, should you choose to send it, will be touched by your thoughtfulness and will appreciate your words more than you know. On the flip side, if there's a relationship that's strained or one that maybe you've already moved on from but you're still harboring a bit of resentment toward that person, consider writing a forgiveness letter. It's advised to not send this letter; rather, you can lean on it as a way to let go and move forward, versus holding on to a relationship that's no longer in your best interest. You can find templates at www.shebelievedbook.com/resources.

Before we wrap up the personal relationships portion of this chapter, we need to pause for a moment and think about the relationships we have and complete a social circle audit.

Who are the top 5–10 people in your inner circle? List them and answer the following questions:

- Are they authentic and genuine?
- Do they fully support you?
- Do you fully support them?
- Do they hold you back because you're chasing dreams that are unfamiliar or evolving into a version of yourself that affects their perception of you?
- Are they cheering you on or speaking limiting beliefs into your mind?

All of these questions and prompts are really important to ask yourself now and in the future.

Leveling Up Professionally

In addition to our romantic, social, and familial relationships, it's critically important to surround yourself with those who can help you get to where you want to go or help you navigate uncharted waters because they've experienced them before. This is critically important in our professional lives, where there are a number of relationships that play a central role in supporting us.

Be Intentional about Your Board of Advisors

It's been reinforced in countless books, by my mentors and coaches and through lived experiences, that we have to be incredibly selective about who we let influence us throughout every stage and phase of our lives and careers. I love the term *board of advisors* when it comes to the influential seats at your table. We choose whom we allow in and how we respond, and it's important to remember that influence is powerful. I've been incredibly intentional about the people I invite in and whose opinions I lean on and when. It's easy to want to seek validation from our social circles but if they haven't walked the walk, or talked the talk, you need to limit how their opinions affect your decisions. That's an even bigger reason to call in the professionals and create a support system around you. I'm cautious to take advice from someone who hasn't done what I am trying to do, and I don't hesitate to surround myself with others who are chasing dreams. This is because I firmly believe that when you surround yourself with those who fully understand and appreciate the investment of time, energy, and effort you're making, because they are also investing in themselves, there's a different level of support, camaraderie, and respect. That type of high-vibe energy and belief is exactly what is needed and required if you want to achieve abundant success in business and life.

Now let me be super clear: you need to get serious about mentorship, personal and professional development, and building your network of professional relationships as you navigate your career or business. All of these lean on your ability to create relationships that matter. The saying "your network equals your net worth" didn't come to be by accident. There are centuries of stories available that touch on the necessity of surrounding yourself with the right people, with the right intentions, as you continue to level up.

Mentorship Matters

When I was newly in recovery from my eating disorders and had decided that I wanted to dedicate my life to helping others, I intentionally sought out mentors in the industry who could help me figure out how to best use my passion, purpose, and time to make a difference. I'll never forget my bold, 18-year-old self, walking up to Lynn Grefe, the newly minted CEO of the National Eating Disorders Association (NEDA), at a conference and sharing with her, out of nowhere, that one day I hoped to be her and would love to have her job. That was very much out of character for me, especially at this time in my life, but to this day I smile when I think about that moment. It was the day that I set the intention that I wanted this woman as my mentor, even though I am sure at the time that she thought I was a bit crazy. Our mentor-mentee relationship took longer than that to develop, but let me tell you, she has absolutely changed my life.

As I proved my dedication and commitment to my passion, the mission of NEDA, and the recovery community, Lynn would advise, guide, and support me in taking on new roles and responsibilities. She gave me a seat at a table that didn't exist prior and offered me the opportunity to build the Junior Board for NEDA from scratch, which was a group of up-and-coming leaders under 40 who were fiercely committed to helping those struggling and their families. After leading that board for three years, and Lynn teaching me how to effectively govern, recruit and fundraise, I was invited to join the national board of directors. I was at least 20 years younger than any of my counterparts but was well equipped to serve in that capacity, thanks to the guidance and mentorship of Lynn. Not only did I have a seat at that table, too, but also I had the opportunity to use my voice and serve in a meaningful way for an additional seven years. Lynn instilled a level of confidence in me that is indescribable and is a perfect example of borrowed confidence because there were many times that I wondered if I should be in those board rooms at all. She saw within me things I couldn't see in myself and nurtured my talents in order to align them with where she saw an opportunity. She was always leveraging her personal Rolodex to make introductions and connections, and never hesitated to challenge my limiting beliefs. Lynn cared deeply about our relationship, as did I, and when she passed away from cancer, the void in my life was very real. She had taken me under her wing, helped to cultivate my passion for the cause, and was always teaching me something, whether or not I wanted to be taught at the time.

What Lynn did for me lit a spark in me to do the same for others. For years, and still, to this day, I mentor young women who have big goals and dreams for themselves, especially when it comes to trailblazing and creating new lanes. I've also continued to place tremendous value on the mentors in my life who guide, support, and oftentimes challenge me to elevate how I am showing up and what goals I am chasing. They also help me truly appreciate the journey I've experienced, reminding me that I need to celebrate the wins, no matter the size, every step of the way.

I encourage you that if you don't already have a mentor to give some thought to who you need in your life right now, and maybe even a little bit farther out in the future. And remember, you're never too old or too young to have one or be one, so please don't let your numerical age limit your ability to be influenced by someone else in a positive way. It can be incredibly beneficial to seek out mentors within your workplace or industry as well as those outside. Be mindful that just like every relationship, it goes both ways. Always seek to be helpful to your mentor as well, and always show gratitude and appreciation for the time they spend with you. And remember, as you evolve, what you need from a mentor will also. Be prepared for this and don't be afraid to reevaluate your needs. They can always remain a friend, but the role of mentor in your life might need to be reassigned as you take on new projects, roles, or responsibilities.

Coaches, Consultants, and Trainers

By now, I am certain that you know that I am a massive fan of investing in yourself and your dreams because you have this incredible potential that deserves to be optimized. We all only have one chance at this game of life, and you should be treating your time as precious moments with unlimited opportunities. And just like any world-class athlete invests in coaching and training, you should too, because you are *world class*.

The coaches, consultants, and trainers who have been or that are in my life currently have made such a significant impact on my outcomes that I am 1,000% certain that I would be nowhere near where I am right now without them. They helped me elevate personally and professionally in ways I could not have imagined. They held me accountable and added rocket fuel to my goals. They opened my eyes to possibilities that I would have never even thought of had I not intentionally invited them into my life and career. They guided me through my own transformation and helped me get out of my own way, especially in the most challenging times, which was usually right before a major breakthrough. I'll forever be grateful to Cynthia Johnson, who throughout the time that we were working on upleveling and redefining my own brand also became a friend and sounding board as I realized that there were even bigger dreams that needed to be chased. And although we got a lot of work done and goals checked off the list, she created a lot of space for me to reflect on where I was versus where I wanted to be. Those conversations coupled with self-reflection have led to amazing results. When I shared with her several years ago that writing a book was a dream of mine, she helped me lay the groundwork so it could be a reality. In addition to Cynthia, Beth Maynard will forever be another strong female role model who was definitely meant to be a part of my life beyond the professional relationship that prompted our initial connection. I initially hired Beth to help us reconfigure our sales organization to meet the ever-growing need and demand we were experiencing. Little did I know that was the beginning of a beautiful friendship that would lead to not only countless memories but also opening the doors and introductions to others that have changed the trajectory of my life. If it were not for Beth, it's highly likely my book dream would not have panned out in the beautiful way that it has as she made the connections and introductions that resulted in this opportunity.

Beth, Cynthia, and many others over the years have held my hand, literally and figuratively, through the darkest times and were the loudest cheerleaders as I took brave, bold action. And although, yes, I was paying them to be a part of my team, they became close friends and deeply invested in my success. There were definitely moments, especially right before signing a contract or investing in a new package, when the fear-based thoughts of "is this going to be worth it?" would creep in, but I've pushed through and taken the plunge more often than not because I vetted them, trusted my gut, and knew that at the end of the day it was up to me to implement what I learned. The return on investment has been life changing for me, both financially and internally, as I have gotten stronger, more resilient, become a better leader, overcome limiting beliefs, and learned how to leverage who I am at my core to be the best version of myself. That type of return is priceless and a major reason I love being a coach and consultant as well. It's about the transformation and elevation for me as I watch my clients truly take ownership of who they are, and what they want, and ultimately get results they never thought possible.

Now you might be saying, "Allison, it takes resources to do this," and, yes, it does. But again, this comes back to choices. I would much rather invest money into someone pouring into me who is helping me grow than in a material item. We will discuss this in more detail as we dive into your goals, but a personal development plan and budget are required for next-level results. Plus, when you have skin in the game, meaning you're spending money on your goals, it increases the likelihood that you will show up for yourself. "Chasing the bag" has become a popular phrase, and although I *love* nice things, too, no one can ever take knowledge, education, or wisdom away from you, so I encourage you to focus on your own evolution and mastery of your skill sets if you're having to choose between your own growth versus your accumulation of items. Personal and professional development has meant so much to me over the years, that even in the more challenging times, I did whatever I could to continue to invest in my dreams. If there's one thing I am willing to bet on, it's myself, and that's one of my driving forces in writing this book.

Rewinding to when I was reinventing my coaching and consulting business in 2015 after Jennifer and I wound down McKenna Walsh, I needed to learn new skills, redefine who I wanted to serve, and understand how to run a profitable online coaching business. I didn't want to make costly mistakes trying to figure it out on my own and was on the hunt for people and programs that had done what I was trying to do. I was also pregnant with my second child and had serious thoughts about not returning to Advanced Recovery Systems (ARS) once maternity leave was over. Because there was so much uncertainty and I was still so risk averse from when we lost almost everything in the 2008/2009 recession, I didn't want to tap into our own savings to finance this new dream.

I'll never forget cleaning out my closet and selling handbags, jewelry, and *so many* clothes that I had accumulated over the years in order to afford to pay for two coaching programs to help me learn what I needed to learn. I took every penny and invested it into myself and my business because I knew at my core that I was worth it. And although I *loved* coaching and would at times joke that I would do it for free, I wanted this to be a real business with real profits, not a hobby, which meant learning new ways of structuring what I offer from coaches who have grown their businesses to seven- and eight-figure companies serving a similar clientele as I was hoping to. The sacrifices I made back then made a massive difference while allowing me to learn new skills and get connected to a community of *amazing* women who were also growing, changing, and stretching in their lives and businesses.

I share regularly that I am always surrounded by support, and honestly I can't imagine trying to figure everything out on my own. I'm grateful that ARS has invested in me over the years, but even if it's not in the budget on that side, I continue to invest in myself year after year because I adopted an "I'm worth it" mentality.

In addition to business coaches, I've also prioritized every area that I wanted to uplevel in. Everything from taking amazing courses through Harvard Business School Online and similar platforms to working with incredible leadership coaches such as Dr. Laura Gallaher, positive psychology coaches including Niyc Pidgeon and Mel Deague, sales trainers such as Beth Maynard, and brand gurus such as Cynthia Johnson and Kristen Hartnegel. I'm never shy to ask for help. After all, athletes never win championships without coaches and trainers, so why would I ever think I could accomplish the goals I have set for myself in the time intended if I didn't surround myself with coaches, too?

The Power of a Mastermind

Napoleon Hill is credited with opening millions of people's eyes and minds to the power of a mastermind. In *Think and Grow Rich*,[3] he introduces the concept of a "master mind alliance" and goes on to describe this group as "a friendly alliance with one or more persons who will encourage one to follow through with both plan and purpose."

The power of a mastermind cannot be understated. When you gather individuals with similar interests, drive, and motivation, with different life experiences and wisdom together, and

---

[3]Hill, N. (2023). *Think and grow rich*. Hilltop Publications.

create the space to learn, grow, and strive for more together, it can change your life.

One of the reasons that these types of relationships and groups have been so successful and impactful in people's lives goes back to early in this chapter when we were discussing how it can be challenging to keep moving forward when those around you are not. By finding "your people" in a mastermind group, you're getting connected with others who have similar interests, and that type of connection alone enables you to show up how you are, as who you are, while giving and receiving feedback with the best of intentions.

Although most mastermind groups have a fee attached to them these days, there's nothing stopping you from seeking out like-minded people, creating the space, and prompting the conversations that are beneficial to those in attendance. There are also a ton of groups on Facebook and LinkedIn that you can join that might introduce you to masterminds, cohorts, or networking groups to start with. And although I know it can be intimidating to show up someplace where you might not know a single soul, that could be exactly the right move and what you need right now.

Relationship with Yourself

Other than your relationship with God or Source, the *most* important relationship you have is the one you have with yourself. I can't beg you enough to prioritize the way in which you take care of yourself and appreciate the magnificence that you possess. The only way for you to truly maximize your potential, enjoy the life you've got, and truly tap into your unique gifts is if you take care of yourself. If you want to show up as the best version of yourself for others, you need to honor, trust, and respect yourself first. This means making time for self-care, practicing self-compassion, setting boundaries, and taking care of your own needs. When you nurture yourself first, you'll be better equipped to nurture your relationships with others. You have to intentionally take care of yourself, especially during challenging seasons, if you want to truly be able to enjoy all that life has to offer. You must practice love and kindness, and mute your inner critic as much as possible, because it's really hard to do the things you need to do for you when self-destructive thoughts are raging. If you notice that negative thoughts are on repeat or that you're neglecting your own needs, pause and be intentional about what you do next.

Consider taking time to journal these thoughts through a letter of compassion where you list out how you're judging yourself or beating yourself up. Once acknowledged, freewrite all of the ways that you can be gentle and extend compassion to yourself. Take a moment to think about issues you may be dealing with and intentionally cultivate self-compassion. Write freely about any thoughts that come into mind—how can you forgive yourself rather than dwell on your mistakes or inadequacies. I want you to speak kindly as if addressing an innocent child instead of beating yourself down further. Inner peace comes from allowing love and forgiveness within—extend compassion toward yourself so that joy can fill your heart. I've included journal prompts and templates for you at www.shebelievedbook.com/resources.

Trust me, I know how difficult this can be, especially if you consider yourself a high achiever who feels like there's always more that could or should be done, but I promise that you will be able to accelerate faster and shine brighter if you're honoring your internal and external needs and taking care of yourself first. We talked about it before, but I believe repetition is best, especially when it pertains to how you take care of yourself. Allow these chapters to reinforce the message that you matter, you are enough, and you deserve the time and space to take care of yourself.

As we wrap up our discussion on relationships, I hope that you pause for the cause and really give sincere consideration to whom you allow into your inner circle and board of advisors. Whom do you need right now? What relationships need to change? Who needs to be added to help you continue to go after what's next in your life and career? Don't make it harder on yourself because you continue to allow negative influences in, or slow your progress by not investing in yourself. I encourage you to make a list of the areas of priority in your life, and who, if anyone, would be beneficial to involve in your journey to help you get from where you are now to where you want to be. Complete the diagram in Figure 6.1, which is also available at www .shebelievedbook.com/resources, to help identify who is currently influencing and affecting your life and career and who may be missing.

Don't hesitate to seek out support, dedicate the resources you need, and don't be afraid to step outside your comfort zone

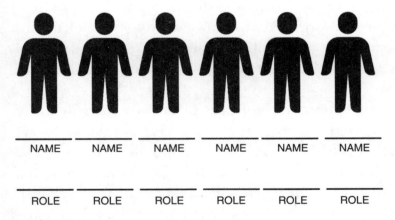

FIGURE 6.1   Your board of advisors.

to meet people who will inspire and invest their time in you in ways you don't even realize yet.

Finally, and most important, do a pulse check on your relationship with yourself. Be honest, and rate yourself on a scale of 1–10, with 10 being the best it could be and 1 being the worst. If it's not what you want it to be, what are you going to commit to doing to change that? As we move into the next chapter and I encourage you to get clear on your goals, it may make sense to include relationships as an area of focus. No matter what, I urge you to give yourself the time necessary to truly take a step back, evaluate the relationships in your life, and create a plan if needed to make positive changes to propel you forward.

Achieve Abundant Success

7

Get Strategic
Set and Achieve Meaningful Goals

When I initially started the book-writing process, I was seriously considering writing an entire book on the power, impact, importance, and science of goal setting, so as I am sure you can imagine, I am fired up for this chapter. Setting the right goals can transform your mindset, approach, and, most important, your outcomes. The truth is, if you don't set goals, it makes it extremely difficult to measure your progress or success. When you have a core area to focus on, goals help you define your areas of focus and give you a guiding light. They help you to also put up blinders for anything that's out of alignment with your priorities. It's extremely easy to get distracted by shiny objects, other opportunities, or the next (and most likely less challenging) thing on your list. Setting goals is an intentional reminder and barometer as to where you should spend your time and energy, because success doesn't happen by accident. Goals are a necessary part of your success equation, so we're going to focus on learning how to effectively set and accomplish goals that will propel you forward and help you achieve your next level of success.

Goal setting is one of my absolute favorite things to work on with individuals at all stages of life and business because it has an immediate and long-term impact that results from taking action and making progress. I've seen a massive transformation happen in countless people's lives, and my own, as a direct result of getting clear on goals and going for them. In addition to the obvious benefits, those who partake in the goal-setting process and consistently gain traction, regardless of whether they reach their ultimate goal, develop grit, resilience, and confidence along the way. All that being said, I am not immune to the reality that the vast majority of well-intended goals, resolutions, and intentions go by the wayside, oftentimes leaving people feeling defeated, disappointed, and uninspired to try again. I'm sure it doesn't come as a shock to you that the most common time of year for individuals to set goals is the new year. Data shows that 80% of those who set New Year's resolutions end up giving up on them by February. My hope is that you learn effective strategies in this chapter that will help you, and those you share them with, to not cancel on your goals and dreams ever again. Your goals matter, and it's time to take action to bring them to fruition. I'm excited for you to put your blinders on, keep your mindset strong, and make the moves you need to in order to evolve, thrive, and possibly defy your own expectations.

You're Never Too Young or Old to Set Goals

I am so grateful that I was introduced to goal setting at a very young age, thanks to Joyce Perrone, one of my coaches. She encouraged me to sit down every New Year's Eve and outline what I wanted to accomplish the following year. I was instructed to write three short-term goals and three long-term goals that would force me to stretch to be a better version of myself. The short-term goals were intended to be able to be completed within three to six months, and the long-term goals could be greater than six months to a year. Once signed off by Joyce, those goals were written on a business card-size piece of paper, laminated, and kept in my wallet the entire year. I *loved* being able to cross things off as they got achieved and the constant reinforcement of seeing them day in and day out in my wallet served as a valuable reminder that I was working on something that mattered to me. It became something I looked forward to each and every year.

When Jennifer and I started McKenna Walsh Coaching and Professional Management and developed our curriculum, goal setting was an exercise we completed with every single client so we were crystal clear on what we were focused on accomplishing during our time together. That exercise has continued to evolve through Allison Walsh Consulting and the She Believed She Could community, as I have coached and trained thousands of ambitious women, both individually and through online training and webinars, helping them to set and achieve their goals. In fact, the number one reason that clients continue to renew and keep me on retainer year after year, and goal after goal, is that I hold them accountable and help them get out of their own way to accomplish what's most important to them. They know that I will show up each and every session and jump in immediately with a status update request on our targeted area of focus. And the same goes for my team as well. As I built our national business development team from the ground up at Advanced Recovery Systems (ARS), I rolled out quarterly goals with monthly accountability meetings and weekly one-on-ones to ensure that we were always focused on hitting our next milestones individually and collectively as a team. It's no surprise that the teams with the greatest levels of clarity, focus, intention, and discipline were the ones consistently on the top of the leaderboard. It solidified the truth that what gets measured gets accomplished, and I hope you're getting excited about what implementing some of these strategies will do for you, too.

Now I'd be lying if I said it was always a pleasant experience. The whole point of setting goals is to push you to do something you either haven't done before, something you want to improve, or something you want to maintain. I tend to lean toward the "haven't done before" category, meaning I live outside my comfort zone the majority of the time, which can be a combination of exciting and terrifying. As I got older and my goals got bigger, I noticed that if there wasn't thoughtful identification of the why and planning for how, the goal would be much more challenging to achieve. I knew I couldn't be the only one who experienced this, so I studied countless high performers, high achievers, and uber-successful people, trying to identify core themes and approaches that would help me, my clients, and my team navigate uncharted waters. In addition to reading and listening to every expert on the subject matter that I could find, I spent thousands of hours with my clients and team members setting goals, mapping out game plans, and, most important, getting the majority of them across the finish line. And, of course, the education received thanks to positive psychology was the cherry on top and further solidified that setting goals isn't good enough. It really comes down to the process, mindset, and approach that's going to determine whether or not something happens. Goal setting and achievement fall within the accomplishment pillar of positive psychology and will be consistently referenced throughout the rest of this book, because this will set the stage as you consider the areas of your life and business that you want to elevate so you can maximize your potential. I'll share with you the research behind goal setting and achievement, along with additional tools that you can use and implement to enhance your own goal achievement statistics.

My intention for you is that you open your mind to new twists on potentially familiar concepts, expand your mindset to unlock your ability to think bigger, and become a goal setter and achiever. My hope is that this chapter enriches your mind and helps you embrace an abundant growth mindset, inspires you to level up because you're deeply connected to the purpose behind your intention, and equips you with memorable frameworks that help you set and achieve any goal you commit to.

Mindset Matters

Before we jump in too deeply on the strategy behind goal setting and achievement, I want to provide some additional context regarding mindset and what needs to happen before goals are identified.

In 2002, Charles R. Snyder, an American professor who specialized in positive psychology, proposed that there are two obstacles that get in the way of us achieving our goals: (1) not believing we can reach the heights of our potential and (2) forgetting how much control—and therefore ease—we have over achieving those aspirations.[1]

Taking it further, renowned author and mindset expert Carol Dweck clearly identifies that people tend to fall into one of two categories when it comes to their mindset, which has a direct correlation to how they live their lives and tackle goals. In her best-selling book *Mindset*, Dweck discusses fixed mindsets versus growth mindsets and the impact of each on one's ability to succeed.[2]

---

[1]Snyder, C. (2002). Hope theory: Rainbows in the mind. *Psychological Inquiry*, *13*, 249–275.
[2]Dweck, C. S. (2008). *Mindset*. Ballantine Books.

Those with fixed mindsets believe that your qualities are carved in stone and tend to not lean into opportunities for personal and professional development. They cap their own potential and stunt their growth because of their own self-imposed limitations. I've seen this also surface when goals are being attempted and a curveball is thrown during the process. People with fixed mindsets have a hard time with divergent thinking, meaning seeing multiple pathways to accomplish their goal, and can easily give up if the linear path is no longer an option.

Those with growth mindsets believe in constant development and are rooted in the belief that your basic qualities are things you can cultivate through your efforts. They enjoy challenges and are much more likely to take risks and stretch themselves because they believe that they'll learn and grow through the process and that every experience is valuable thanks to the lessons that will be learned.

Depending on your mindset, you'll approach challenges, handle setbacks, and view outcomes (or the lack thereof) differently. It's important to recognize and identify early on if your mindset is potentially limiting your success. I highly encourage you to really take a step back and evaluate where you fall on the spectrum of fixed mindset versus growth mindset. I've included a link at www.shebelievedbook.com/resources to take the Growth Mindset quiz to determine where you are so you know how to proceed.

Once you've evaluated your mindset, ask yourself these questions:

- Is your mindset something that needs attention?

- Can you challenge yourself to grow by stepping outside of your comfort zone by trying new things or learning new skills?

- Would it benefit your life to shift more in the growth mindset direction to help you level up in all areas of your life?

I believe that you picked up this book for a reason, so I am going to assume that you are already leaning toward the growth mindset side of the spectrum. And because I know you are focused on reaching your next level of success, we are going to jump right into how to make those big, bold, dreams of yours a reality.

SMART Goals

I've always been a huge fan of SMART goals, meaning those that are specific, measurable, achievable, relevant, and time bound. This still leaves room for error and overwhelm, but it serves as a great starting point, so we're going to review each of these five areas before we supercharge this approach with three additional areas of focus that will increase your likelihood of achieving your goals. I've included worksheets at www.shebelievedbook.com/resources to help you define and articulate your goals.

Specific

The more specific and concrete your goal is, the easier it will be for you to create a laser-focused approach to achieving it. Over the years, I've seen so many people struggle with specificity and really drilling down to what it is that they want to accomplish. Consider the *S* of the SMART goal framework to be the mission statement of your goal. Do not be vague in the language you're using when defining your goal. It can be very helpful to consider the who, what, when, where, why, and how as you create your goal. Digging deeper enables you to get more specific, thus enhancing the quality of the goal you're achieving. Let's use the example of writing this book for purposes of clarity. If I approached the goal to "write a book in 2023" as I just wrote it, it's missing so many elements that will enhance the likelihood of me actually making it happen. It's missing any specific details about what it's about, for whom, the why behind it, and a specific time frame. I could easily upgrade this goal by reframing it to "Write a 50,000-word business success book in 12 weeks to help people improve their mindset, confidence, and ability to achieve their goals."

Measurable

As previously mentioned, what gets measured gets accomplished. Do not be afraid to attach numbers, benchmarks, and measurements of success to your goals. In my opinion, this is one of the most useful and important aspects of your goal. Coupled with time bound, you can break down the numerical targets to align with the designated amount of time that you're allocating for the goal to be achieved. In my experience, when this is missing from a goal, either the individual doesn't realize its importance or they're dodging accountability.

Focusing on how we are going to measure the progress of a goal during the goal formation process also helps with not attaching too much to a singular goal. I oftentimes see people bake way too many elements into a singular goal, get overwhelmed by the magnitude, and then quit on themselves. The better approach is to make smaller, more micro-goals that stack up to a larger goal than to bite off more than you can chew in a singular goal.

If we're looking at the example "Write a 50,000-word business success book in 12 weeks to help people improve their mindset, confidence, and ability to achieve their goals," the measurable metric that will help me achieve the book-writing process is the word count. The word count coupled with a time frame will enable me to create an action plan.

Achievable

The achievable element is an opportunity for you to evaluate whether or not you're capable of getting a goal across the finish line. A challenging, yet realistic goal should encourage you to stretch, potentially learn new things, or step up your game. An unachievable goal and one that should be reconsidered would be something that is unrealistic or too far out of reach. Please listen when I say that you don't want to set yourself up for failure right out of the gate. There's a big difference between ambitious, realistic goals and those that are far too extreme for this phase and stage of your life. As I set my writing goals for this book, I looked at what I was currently doing, and what was going to be required to complete the manuscript. I was averaging about 1,000/words per day, so I knew that 5,000 words per week was a realistic target. I built in two weeks of buffer time to give myself grace and space to account for unexpected challenges (which there ended up being), barriers, or any writer's block that I might experience. I checked the calendar and cross-referenced life obligations and determined that 50,000 words within 12 weeks was achievable. Me going through that exercise of evaluating whether or not this was possible gave me the confidence to go all in, and I encourage you to do the same. As you set and map your goals, it is important to check them to make sure that it is actually possible, even if it feels outside of your comfort zone.

Relevant

I like to refer to the relevant portion of SMART goals as the "what's the point" part of the equation. Relevance refers to focusing on something that makes sense within the grander scheme of the broader goals you have for your life, career, or in business. For example, if writing a 50,000-word business success book was not in alignment with my overall mission, it shouldn't be a priority or take up space on my calendar. Ideally, each goal should help you get closer to your overall mission and vision that you have for yourself.

Time Bound

When you consider time, I encourage you to think about the parameters that you are carving out to achieve your goals. I can't stress this enough because without it there are no defined points in which you're striving for completion. Without a target completion date, it makes it difficult to define appropriate times to measure and pulse check your progress. If I didn't put a 12-week timeline on my book writing process, I would struggle to divide up the necessary word count per week. Personally, I know that I would have a harder time staying disciplined and on a writing schedule if there weren't a time period attached to when the manuscript would be due to the publisher. As a side note, I highly encourage you to use a 90-day time frame as often as appropriate. The reason for this is that it enables you to hyper-focus on getting goals across the finish line while staying nimble enough to adjust to any unforeseeable roadblocks. Although some goals might not take that long, and others may require more time, I've seen far more individuals be successful using 90-day sprints to achieve their goals than those who do not. Plus, it enables you to focus on four significant goals per year rather than stretching them out, potentially losing momentum, and not achieving what you set out to do if you allowed for more time than is truly necessary to achieve the goal.

I encourage you to spend time thinking about what type of goals would be meaningful to set for your life and career. Here are examples of SMART goals that some of my clients set this year:

- I want to launch my online consulting business and have three paying clients within the next 90 days.
- I want to launch my personal brand via Instagram, Facebook, and my new personal website within the next 90 days.

- I want to finish my manuscript in six months so that I can self-publish within the next 12 months.

- I want to scale my personal brand and online influence by increasing my social media followers on Instagram from 5,000 to 10,000 over the next three months.

- I want to increase my gross revenue by $10,000/month within the next six months.

How to W.I.N. When Setting Goals

Now that you have the basic SMART goal framework, it's time to kick it up a few notches. Consider the next framework as a way to supercharge your ability to reach any goal you set your mind to. When I started introducing this to my clients and team members, it was remarkable how helpful it was because it enabled us to connect every goal to a why, define the intentional efforts that would be made, and encourage a new level of commitment and attitude by each and every one of them by agreeing to a no excuses mentality. But before I dive in too deep, I want to first share with you how this supplemental framework made all of the difference as I implemented it during an incredibly challenging time.

When I started building the team at ARS, we wanted to be multisite, multistate, and save thousands of lives each year in our centers. Every year we were given annual, quarterly, monthly, weekly, and even daily targets that we needed to hit in order to be able to achieve the growth we were hoping for.

Toward the end of 2019, we were on a solid run. We had gained a lot of momentum and had continued to open centers every year. There were two major joint ventures in motion with hospital systems in Florida and New Jersey, the pipeline was full of additional exciting opportunities, and our dreams of building a company valued over a billion dollars weren't too far out of reach. I remember being so lit up at the thought of being able to make major things happen for the company. At this point, we had grown to more than 1,000 team members and nine locations in six states and additional centers were coming online soon. So many things were going right and we were really well positioned to make dreams come true and save a lot of lives in the process.

Then, COVID-19 rocked our worlds.

As the coronavirus made its way to the United States, we braced ourselves for impact. ARS has two locations in Washington State, the site of the country's first recognized COVID outbreak, so we were keenly aware that something was going to have to be done sooner rather than later. We temporarily paused admissions but I don't think any of us anticipated what would happen next.

In mid-March 2020, our founder and CEO called an emergency meeting with our team. We were temporarily stopping *all* admissions into our centers as we wrapped our heads around what we were going to do next. We were to cut back our budgets by at least 30%, and our leadership team would be taking a significant reduction in salary to hopefully ease the impact of the uncertain times ahead. Our new goals centered on being able to stay operational and safe, versus scaling and selling.

At that very moment, I sat in utter disbelief. For the next several days we had to make awful calls. I had to let a significant portion of my team go, which was absolutely heartbreaking. On those calls, I promised each of them that I would do everything in my power to be able to call them back and welcome them back as soon as possible.

Because we could no longer generate business as usual, which for my team meant six to eight meetings per day with referral sources and accounts, we had to transition to a fully virtual sales team and create new key performance indicators that would help us adapt to a new sales process in a very short period of time. In addition, many of our referral sources were not able to sustain the impact of COVID-19, so we had the increasing pressure of generating new business while also trying to sustain what was left. My incredibly resilient field team pivoted and each of them made the conscious decision to put their foot on the virtual gas. Each of them went from dialing 100 times a week to 100 times a day. We quickly implemented a video platform so they could stand out among the thousands of competitors filling up our accounts and prospects' inboxes. We were also one of the first in our space to pivot our in-person events to online so we were able to rapidly increase our reach and provide a best-in-class experience yielding new leads and opportunities for the team.

Very few of my team loved executing this new plan, but they loved saving lives, which was the ultimate goal of our work. The thought that their commitment could help bring their other team members back was added jet fuel for many of them. It certainly was for my day in and day out as I navigated the unknown.

This experience reinforced a core principle for me—and something that often gets overlooked—it doesn't matter how good your goals are if you don't have a deep connection to them. As I looked at what we were attempting to accomplish, I knew we needed more than targets to hit.

Your *Why* Matters

The foundation of the WIN framework is your *why*. I've consistently noticed that if someone can't pinpoint exactly why their goal matters to them, they have a much harder time staying motivated during the goal achievement process. In positive psychology, there's a lot of discussion in the Meaning pillar about the importance of working toward goals that are meaningful and enable you to stay connected to your purpose. Studies have shown that to have a sense of meaning, we need to feel that what we do is valuable and worthwhile. This involves belonging to and/or serving something that we believe is greater than ourselves.[3]

Purpose, however, is about action and moving toward an overarching mission and goal. Emily Smith's research suggests that people who have a purpose believe that their lives are more meaningful and more satisfying, and as a result, they're more resilient and motivated to work through challenges that present themselves.[4] Professor Michael Steger's studies suggest that you're likely to feel happier, more motivated, committed, and more satisfied when you can find a sense of meaning in your work and what you do.[5] Although not every goal you go after will always light up your meaning and purpose, those that do will likely be accomplished far more than those that do not.

As you define your goal, consider these questions:

- Why does this goal matter to you?
- Why do you want to accomplish it?
- What does accomplishing this goal mean for your future self?

In addition to connecting your goals to a strong why, positive psychology supports the idea that agency thinking, or the motivation that moves people toward their goals, is incredibly important. Agency thinking is made up of thoughts related to beliefs individuals have about themselves being able to start working on a goal, continue progressing until it's reached, and finally experience the success they've been striving for.

---

[3]Seligman M. E. P. (2011). *Flourish*. Simon & Schuster.
[4]Smith, E. E. (2017). *The power of meaning: Creating a life that matters*. Broadway Books.
[5]http://www.michaelfsteger.com/

During the pandemic, the why for many of us at ARS included not only keeping our jobs and saving the company we had built from scratch but also honoring our deep connections to our colleagues and bringing our team back together. Every time we hit new targets, I would get to make a call and invite someone back to the team. Nothing was better than seeing them on the next team call and watching their colleagues beam, knowing full well that their commitment and belief in their ability to rebuild enabled us to bring the person back. We did a lot of things we didn't want to do to get the results we weren't sure we would get. Field reps in general thrive off of being around people and building relationships face-to-face. My team literally increased their output by five times what we had initially planned for when we started 2020. They worked long days and pushed through countless months of uncertainty, trusting deep down that we would and could make it through. The fact that they were able to adjust and do business differently for 18 months following the initial shutdown, and do so effectively is something I will admire for years to come. Despite all of the hurdles, we kept going day by day as we continued to forge ahead together.

This experience reinforces the idea that the why behind your goal might have to remain fluid to account for variables that were not anticipated or expected. Although my initial why of hustling to build this incredible team was connected to my desire to affect people's lives in significant ways while making an income, during the days, months, and years of the pandemic, it shifted to preserving our team, securing the company's future, and making sure that we could continue our mission. Ultimately and most important, you must stay intrinsically connected to why you're tackling your goal if you want to achieve it, which means you might have to re-evaluate why you're striving for that goal if you notice motivation is waning. I encourage you to consistently check in with yourself and how you're feeling toward the goal you are chasing. Are you connected to a why that is powerful enough to motivate you on the days you don't want to do the work that will get you closer to your destination?

Intention

Now that we understand the importance of why, it's time to get intentional about the goal you've defined for yourself. When you approach your goals with intention, discipline, and action, truly anything is possible. First and foremost, once you have your SMART goal defined, you must create an action plan. You can't just set the goal and expect it to happen. It's also extremely helpful if you break your SMART goal into a series of micro-goals, that when accomplished, will enable you to achieve the overall goal.

Using my book example, the daily writing goal is one of the ways I was intentional about this process. The next was carving out the time to make it happen. I knew I needed dedicated, uninterrupted time for myself in order to write. I also knew how long it would take me to write each day, in addition to the other tasks that were still on my plate, and I recognized that I am at my best in the morning. This meant that I had to find 60–90 minutes before the craziness of the day began that was all mine. Taking it another step further, I was keenly aware that if I didn't preplan the night before about what I was going to write about, I would struggle in the morning and most likely get distracted by literally anything else that caught my attention. So the intentional process I put in place to knock out my daily writing responsibilities was as follows:

Night Before

- Make sure my outline or bullet points were identified for the next morning so I don't have to figure out what I need to write about.
- Prep for the morning: lemon water in the fridge and coffee pot set.
- Go to sleep by 9:30 p.m. at the latest so I am fresh in the morning.

Morning

- Rise and shine, drink my lemon water, complete morning meditation/journaling, and a short workout to get the blood flowing.
- Go time! No checking emails or social media until I was done writing.

This schedule provided me with the structure, space, and ability to do what I needed to do before the kids got up and the morning got crazy. Plus, I always felt so good about myself because I honored the commitment I made to *myself* to work on something that matters for my future.

Discipline is what shows up when motivation wants to take a nap.

Although I wish we could always be motivated, there will most likely be days that we are not. This is where the habits you create and how disciplined you are make all the difference. One of my favorite reminders for my team and my community is that discipline is what shows up when motivation wants to take a nap. Your daily, intentional steps forward toward your goal will stack up, but you have to commit to a plan. And please don't underestimate the power of consistency. Consistency compounds and persistency pays off, so stay focused and do what you need to do to get that goal across the finish line. My preplanned daily routine coupled with staying deeply connected to why while writing this book was so important to me. It helped me tremendously on the days when motivation was lagging and the snooze button on my alarm was more enticing than sticking to my routine. I can whole-heartedly attest that my intentional planning, knowing, and acknowledging my potential pitfalls in advance, and honoring my commitment to complete this on time enabled me to show up and do the work. I refused to cancel on this goal and dream because deep down I knew how much it meant to me. I encourage you to set yourself up for success as well by clearly creating the space and time you need to work on your goals, preplan in advance what needs to get done and never lose sight of your why.

No Excuses

At the end of the day, you can have results or excuses, but you can't have both.

The *N* in the WIN framework is for no excuses. Now I realize this might seem harsh, but I will tell you it's a complete game changer when it comes to accomplishing goals and getting results. I would be doing you a complete disservice if we didn't have a heart-to-heart about the barriers and obstacles that we face as we chase and accomplish our goals. At the end of the day, you can have results or excuses, but you can't have both.

Now I understand that in rare circumstances, there will be things that are far too extreme to overcome (unexpected illnesses, accidents, or mental health challenges), but I'm focused more on the daily excuses that creep in and hijack our time. Even worse, these excuses somehow gain traction the longer or more fre-quently that we allow ourselves to co-sign on them. I know that growth, change, leveling up, and stepping outside of your comfort zone can be scary, but what should be scarier is letting your excuses stand between you and your potential.

As you think about the goals that you've set in the past, think about the excuses, objections, or obstacles that have come up. Common ones I hear all of the time are what I call the *not enoughs*, meaning "not enough time," "not enough money," "not enough support," or "not enough knowledge/experience." All of these can be overcome if you plan accordingly and seek out what you need or become more disciplined with your time. Just like you are going to create an action plan thanks to the *I* in WIN, you need to create a plan on how you're going to address the obstacles, excuses, or barriers to your success. The best part about this exercise is that you *know* how you will navigate them, which will give you the confidence to continue to move forward knowing you are prepared if the original plan is faced with challenges. And although you can't always predict potential challenges along the way, chances are you have some awareness of what could pose a threat, delay, or cancellation of your goals coming to fruition. Once you've articulated them and mapped them out just as you've done with the goal itself, it's time to do so for the potential barriers while simultaneously creating a game plan in case you have to adjust your strategy or approach if challenges present themselves. Positive psychology calls this *pathway thinking*, meaning the multiple ways in which you can accomplish the goal you've defined. If you're too linear in your approach, it won't take much to knock you off course when challenges arise. Give yourself the time and space to explore what could get in the way and how you will circumvent those obstacles to keep making forward progress. For example, I knew there could potentially be mornings that I wouldn't be able to write, most likely due to kids not sleeping through the night or other projects that have a shorter deadline and needed to get prioritized. As a result, I knew that I could make up for that time either immediately after work was done for the day or I would plan to hunker down on the weekends while my daughters were practicing at the dance studio. This allowed me to not stress out in the mornings when it was unrealistic for me to squeeze in writing time and give myself grace instead of beating myself up for getting off track. Admittedly I've now written thousands of words from the pink chair in the back corner of the dance studio because I needed to stay on schedule in order to finish my book on time. When you adopt a no excuses mentality you drastically affect your commitment and likelihood of success. Plus you gain ridiculous momentum along the way and the residual impact of your efforts will bless you in ways you don't even realize just yet.

Our pandemic pivot at ARS was and will forever be a permanent reminder for me about how important it was for me as a leader and team member to own my responsibilities and look for multiple ways in which we could achieve our goals. Because of the intentional hustle, drive, and motivation that each and every one of my team members showed up with during the first nine months of the pandemic, not only did we welcome our team members back but the business development team increased our opportunities by 38% from the year prior by the end of 2020. That experience taught us so much about how resilient we were and how so much was possible even when the deck felt as though it was stacked against us. Our blinders-on, mindset-strong mentality, and desire to *win* every day made all the difference. And although there were terribly difficult days and weeks that we encountered, we were always there for each other on the days when we wanted to throw in the towel. We allowed our faith in ourselves and our abilities to be louder than our fears, and every single day we stayed super focused on our *why*, were *intentional* about what we did, and had a *no-excuses* mentality.

13 Steps to Help You Achieve Abundant Success

In addition to using the SMART goals and WIN framework, here are 13 additional tips to help you achieve your goals.

1. **You *must* write them down.** You are 42% more likely to accomplish your goals if they're in writing.[6] It's also incredibly valuable to keep them visible in your workspace or somewhere that you'll see them every day.

2. **Do not tackle too many goals at once.** Instead, carve out dedicated time and space to go after one at a time. For example, if you have four goals you want to achieve during a year, try tackling one every 90 days, instead of all four at once. Chances are you'll make more progress, be less overwhelmed, and gain confidence as you go.

3. **Schedule check-ins on your calendar.** And I do mean put them in your calendar *now*. I have a thorough 90-day goal review every quarter. I also have pulse checks monthly to ensure I am going to hit my targets. From there, it's easy to break the bigger goal into manageable, micro-targets that will add up to success. I've included a link to my 90-day planner at www.shebelievedbook.com/resources.

4. **Commit to daily action.** You do not want to overwhelm yourself with your goals by trying to cram action into the final days of your deadline because it will make it easier for you to bail on them. Instead, do one thing every day that gets you closer to your goals. If you work in 90-day sprints as I do, that's 90 opportunities to make it happen.

5. **Diminish your fear.** Fear plays a major role in even getting started. When you write down what could get in your way,

---

[6] Forbes Books. (2017 July 18). The science of setting goals and achieving them. https://books.forbes.com/author-articles/the-science-behind-setting-goals-and-achieving-them/

you remove it and empower yourself simultaneously. For this, I encourage you to ask yourself, "Why am I feeling this way and what evidence do I have that it will actually happen?" Oftentimes, we allow our fears to dominate our thoughts, but once they're on paper and you've diffused them, you can move through them and keep going.

6. **Get an accountability partner.** You are 60% more likely to see your goals through if you're working on them while paired with an accountability buddy.[7] If you don't know where to turn, join groups online, hire a coach, or enroll in a mastermind where there's a collective group of people working toward their goals.

7. **Have skin in the game.** When you invest in yourself or your goals, your likelihood of actually accomplishing them skyrockets. If, for whatever reason, it's *free*, still pay for it. Move money, or put money into a jar for your next-level investment into your personal and professional development. Psychologically you will be inclined to see it through, and it will sting much more if you don't.

8. **Prioritize. Prioritize. Prioritize.** You have to make sure you make your goals a priority and don't dilute your focus. When you dilute your focus, you dilute your results. If what's on your to-do list is not in alignment with your goals, redo the list. And remember, every time you say yes to someone or something else, you're taking time away from your goals.

9. **See it before it happens.** I am a huge fan of future casting as a source of motivation and inspiration, meaning visualizing myself as having already achieved that goal. I allow myself to think and feel as though it's happened, and focus on what the results mean to my future self. It's also helpful to lean into

---

[7]Wissman, B. (2018 March 20). An accountability partner makes you more likely to succeed. *Entrepreneur*. https://www.entrepreneur.com/article/310062

manifestation practices and use tried-and-true techniques to help you take ownership of the outcome and get excited about what it will do for you. Instead of saying "I hope I am . . ." say "I am . . ." and watch your energy and outcomes shift.

10. **Celebrate milestones.** I can't stress this enough. Life moves fast and as soon as you're close to accomplishing your goal, your mind will probably already be thinking about what's next. Pause. Celebrate. Reflect and *level up*. I also encourage you to celebrate the small wins along the way because otherwise they'll get lost in the shuffle and you'll miss the opportunity to acknowledge your growth.

11. **Audit your outcome.** Not everything will go as planned each and every time. When you pause to evaluate what went well, what didn't, and how you can improve on your next goal sprint, be honest about what you could have done differently. Did you slack on your time management or habits? Do you need a coach, mentor, or course to help you? If so, do the research and make it happen.

12. **Fail fast and fail forward.** It's far better to put your foot on the gas and attempt your goal quickly than to extend the timeline and delay your ability to measure whether or not it was successful. Remember, even if it isn't successful, you are learning and growing in the process, which means the next time that you attempt it, you'll be able to navigate challenges much easier and apply what you've learned to your next try.

13. **Build on momentum.** You taking action and creating results for yourself is invigorating. Do not take your foot off the gas. Action builds momentum and momentum opens doors and opportunities for you that you never thought possible. Now that you have solid new habits, a new level of confidence, and some wins under your belt, it's time to go after the next big goal!

You deserve all of the success you've been dreaming about, but it will not happen by accident.

Your possibilities are endless and your potential is limitless. You will be successful when you remove the excuses and the potential pitfalls and put accountability tools in place. Don't be afraid of writing them down and speaking them into the universe. In fact, that's exactly what you should do. Remember, three months of focus and intentional effort can truly change your life. The time is going to pass anyway, so why shouldn't it be filled with progress, celebrations, and elevation? You deserve all of the success you've been dreaming about, but it will not happen by accident. Go for it. Believe you can. It's your time to shine.

Have you set goals for yourself? Are you dreaming big enough or are you playing small with your goals? Are they in alignment with best practices? How can you adopt the WIN mentality and apply it to your goals?

To download your goal-setting checklist and WIN framework, go to www.shebelievedbook.com/resources.

8

Your Success Routine
Master Your Time Management Skills

Time is the most precious thing you have. Once it's gone, you can't get it back. What you do with your time will determine so many aspects of your life and your ability to be successful. So please, protect your time like the gold it is.

One of the most common questions I get asked is how I manage my time. I have many responsibilities, yet I am always focused on continued growth and development. My schedule requires me to be incredibly disciplined with my time and avoid "time leaks" throughout the day when time is wasted or unaccounted for. I must focus on the intentional prioritization of tasks so I can show up and be as present and productive as possible during the allotted time. Not everything always goes as planned, but because I am crystal clear on how I will *win* the day, it makes it easy for me to reset or adjust my schedule to keep making progress rather than getting sidetracked or delayed.

Before we get in too deep, I want to be transparent: I do not and will not advocate for hustle culture, meaning the 24/7 grind, the sleep-when-you're-dead mentality. In fact, my mission in this chapter is to share with you advice and suggestions that can help you regain time and give you more space to do the things that matter to you. I rely on discipline, intention, and structure in order to create opportunities to do the things that light me up from the inside.

Nothing is more unfulfilling or exhausting than feeling like I am on a hamster wheel or chained to a never-ending to-do list. It can also severely affect creativity and enjoyment and be a fast track to burnout. I learned the hard way how important it is to take extreme ownership of your time and energy and stop giving it away to people, places, and things that are not aligned with where you are headed or what you want.

As I have continued to coach high achievers one-on-one and develop talent within our organization, one of the core areas we focus on is time management. When people come to me for help, my instant response is, "Your success is hidden in your daily routine," so we're going to start there. Calendar reviews, time blocks, and prioritization lead the way, with the desired outcomes and results always at the forefront of our minds. My mission is always to help people find where they are wasting time, regain control over their schedules, get done what needs to be accomplished, decompress so they can enjoy life, and not feel like they're burning the candle at both ends.

A concept I want to address before jumping into a wealth of advice and valuable tips to help you become a time-management maven is work-life balance. Honestly, I think this entire concept has created unrealistic expectations that leave people feeling less than stellar about themselves and their careers on a regular basis.

If ever there was an example of how this warped mindset affected us, it was the pandemic, where for the vast majority of us, balance went out the window. For once, millions of people realized that integration was much more achievable as we juggled competing and conflicting priorities while still being expected to show up and do what we needed to do when we needed to do it. It became that much more important to create boundaries for ourselves in order to shut down, unwind, and not go completely crazy while attempting to juggle it all. Boundaries are beautiful and will enable you to create the life and career that you want by being clear about what is and isn't acceptable, but it's up to you to define them even if integration is what you're striving for. And trust me when I tell you that on the upward climb to success, the value of your time becomes increasingly significant, so you have got to learn how to construct boundaries that support you.

Whether you're an entrepreneur, a stay-at-home parent, working a 9-to-5, or starting a side hustle, the truth is that you have the time, but what you do with it matters. And although I will shout from the rooftops that you *can* have it all, you will have to choose when and how to make your vision come true. I urge you to get selfish about the time you have and stop giving it away if you're in a season of your life where you've got to show up for you to make your dreams happen. Trust me, I know how hard it is, especially if you're a people pleaser like me at your core, but if you want to make big things happen, you cannot let time zappers that are not in alignment with your vision steal your most precious commodity.

My mission is to show you how to be effective with your time and maximize your minutes, so you can optimize the potential of each day. Please do not take any advice to mean you must be working at all hours of the day and running yourself ragged, trying to fit everything in. Instead, spending time here enables you to maximize your time so you can show up in all the places and spaces that matter to you and still make big things happen in life and business.

Get Clear Priorities

If you have more than three priorities, you don't have priorities. We've talked a lot about focus, intention, and avoiding diluting your priorities when you are setting your goals. The same goes for your time, which is the main element when you continue to level up in business and life. Priority identification and alignment can go a long way regarding your ability to streamline how and where you spend your time. Trust me when I say that the more successful you are, the more people will want access to you. Although it can feel good to feel wanted, I want to remind you that every time you say yes to them, you're saying no to yourself. After all, no is a complete sentence and should be used far more often than it is. You must unapologetically prioritize yourself, your needs, and your goals; otherwise, you can quickly lose track of your schedule and time. If it's not a heck, yes, it should be a no. Every opportunity, invitation, and ask should be measured against the priorities you have set for yourself. And let me be crystal clear—you need to identify your priorities. Sure, I understand that if you're working for someone else, they may dictate priorities for you, but ultimately you have the final say with where you spend your time once you've clocked out for the day. Work may be one of the priorities you've established in your life, but if building a side business that can eventually replace that space is also on the list, you've got to carve out the intentional time to work on it. To further demonstrate this, I've had multiple clients whose priorities have revolved around faith, family, and career.

As they established goals, the goals that correlated to their top priorities took precedence over those that did not.

Please pause for a moment and get clear on your top three priorities before we jump in. They're your north star and guiding light for this chapter. It doesn't mean you don't or won't get to enjoy anything beyond your top three. It just means that those will be what take center stage, get scheduled first, and have the appropriate amount of time attached to them so you can bring any goals connected to them to fruition. Write them down here:

Priority 1:

Priority 2:

Priority 3:

Now that you've established your top three, we can do a deep dive into time management to ensure that you have the time and space you need to keep building the life and career of your dreams. I encourage you to do the work in this chapter, because it can significantly affect your personal and professional life. It's an area that needs more attention, and it is my intention to help you regain control over your time so that you can work on what *you* want to work on and not overstretch yourself with obligations that shouldn't be on your list.

Most important, this is your life, and no one understands the depth of your commitments better than you. The beautiful thing about the world we live in now is that we have choices. We can get unstuck if we notice that we don't have enough time or where we spend our time isn't fulfilling. As my dear friend Brian reminds me, "We have choices, and with those choices, we can make decisions. However, those decisions have consequences." The good news is we're in charge, and we can decide to reclaim the time, leverage it as we need, and prioritize our efforts daily.

Time Audits

Whether or not time management and productivity are areas that you're struggling with, I highly encourage you to complete a time audit to see where you're missing out on opportunities to maximize your time or give yourself more space to do things that light you up from the inside. I have to admit, the first time I was asked to do this by my boss, I was insulted, and a bit offended. I didn't think I was wasting time, but I noticed that I was struggling to get everything that needed to be completed done. Now granted, my plate was overfull during that season of life, but it wasn't impossible.

Reluctantly, I tracked my time for two weeks straight, and it turned out my boss was right. I had time leaks all over the place. My biggest takeaways from that experiment helped me restructure my days and consolidate what was soaking up my minutes. Even more so, I was able to create a simple process that enabled me to stay productive even when things changed out of nowhere. The result was getting more done in less time, cutting out things that no longer should be priorities or time zappers, delegating things that took me away from my zone of genius, and mastering my schedule so I didn't feel as overwhelmed or depleted by the end of the day. I then took what I learned and applied it to my consulting business and life overall and allowed myself the chance to recapture the time that wasn't being used effectively so I could, in some ways, multiply the effects of excellent time management and increase not only my earning potential but my sanity as well.

Time audits are simple to complete and eye-opening if you're honest with yourself. I've included a template for you to use at www.shebelievedbook.com/resources, but we're going to pause here with additional details to help conceptualize what I'll reference throughout this chapter.

I consider this mission critical, regardless of your profession, and especially if you're looking to do something new or invest your time, energy, and effort into something that matters to you that doesn't already have dedicated time attached to it.

For the next two weeks, I want you to track everything in 15-minute blocks. This is because meetings or calendar invites often end up on your schedule yet don't take up the entire time. After the two-week challenge, I challenge you to be honest with yourself to see what should remain a 30-minute meeting versus shrinking it to 15 or maybe become an email update instead. I've noticed with so many people, including myself, that scheduled meetings soak up valuable real estate on your calendar, end early, or go longer than they need to, and then you have wasted or unfocused time that isn't leveraged. Although you may not be in control of the calendar invite, and your suggestion to shorten the meeting may not be welcomed, you, as the time-management maven in your life, can immediately pivot to things that can be accomplished during those windows of time rather than delaying progress on other things that matter.

For example, there are two recurring meetings on Wednesday mornings that I have to attend. They account for 9–11 a.m. every week, yet they rarely go past 75 minutes total. Because I know that I'll get time back more often than not, I have an additional block, also known as my pivot list, on my schedule with a list of what I can or should focus on once that meeting wraps. The natural tendency would be to wait until the next meeting at 11 begins to get back on track, but I know that I can bump up other tasks to fill that time, move the needle in the right direction, and potentially allow me to either get more accomplished or end earlier because I was organized and efficient. So on Wednesdays, there is a block that has tasks that I could pivot to that will take no longer than 45 minutes to complete or make headway on. One reason I love digital calendars is that I can slide that invite elsewhere if, for some reason, I don't get that bonus time on my calendar.

This works really well for my field sales team as well. Oftentimes their meetings fluctuate, and they've got spare time between meetings. I encourage them always to have a call list to dial in between so they can maximize their time and not let other people's schedules dictate their productivity. This also enables them to finish their tasks before they make their way home and help minimize what's left on their to-do lists before they can switch gears and spend time with family and friends or do something else that fills up their cups.

Also, once you've done your time audit and you see consistent themes and opportunities, you can leverage that time for restorative breaks or something that recharges you. That bonus time can be exactly what you need, especially if your schedule is tight. Remember, either you run the day or the day runs you. Despite what it may feel like, you are in control of the time you have, and my guess is there's time you can reclaim by completing an audit.

Calendar Everything

Your calendar is sacred. You have 86,400 seconds in a day, many of which are spent resting and recharging, which means when you're awake, a rock-solid plan enhances your productivity and gives you the space to be present wherever you are. I'm sure you're familiar with the quote, "Fail to plan, plan to fail," and in my experience, it's true. We can't be casual about life when we are chasing big goals and dreams, and I hope that you create a schedule that inspires and supports you to give yourself the gift of time to accomplish what you're working on.

Now I don't care if you prefer digital or paper, but you have to have a singular source of truth when it comes to your schedule. I can't even begin to tell you how often I work with people, and they've got several different calendars, countless sticky notes with to-dos, and way more things in their brains taking up space. Add in any parental duties or their kid's extracurriculars, and we've got a recipe for disaster. Once we get everything out of your brain and onto a written or online calendar, you will feel a sense of relief, even if it looks overwhelming.

You must start with your non-negotiables first and build in everything else. This means all of the things you have to do and that matter to you, both personally and professionally. Even more important, try as best as you can to plug things in as soon as you're aware of them, rather than allowing yourself to get double booked and potentially miss out. I don't care if you think it's a minimal task or not necessary to write it down. My intention is for you to assign the time to be completed and accounted for because it will make it much easier for you to evaluate what you really spent your time on during the week the next time you choose to audit your time and productivity.

Win Your Week and Your Days

I encourage you to carve out time on Sunday to plan your week and zoom out to see the bigger picture. Our schedule constantly changes, with three kids and multiple businesses, so planning for my week keeps me much calmer and more present. Communicate with everyone in your world who needs to know what is going on, where you are required, and what support would be helpful to allow you not to get overwhelmed. The goal here is to have *less stress* and enable you to feel in control and at peace. Remember that consistency compounds, and as you adopt a mentality of time spaciousness rather than lack, your anxiety about getting things done will reduce. You control your schedule even if it feels like you don't. Please read that again if you need to. This is *your* life. You are in the driver's seat. You make the decisions about where you spend your time and with whom. I understand that you might not be doing what you want right now, but that means that you need to be a time-management maven to create the space to invest in yourself.

This logic has been incredibly useful for the multi-passionate clients whom I've coached over the years. Many of them have been building their brands or future full-time businesses while they've been working in their 9–5 (or much longer) jobs. Time management was critical, and the time before they clocked in was paramount. Breaking down what needed to happen before they switched gears for the day enabled them to make the necessary progress to continue to make moves.

In addition to mapping and planning out your week, taking a few minutes before you wind down at the end of your day makes a major difference. When you refocus your list and prioritize where you want or need to start the next day, you will be shocked by how much more you accomplish right out of the gate the next day. Plus, you'll put your mind at ease knowing that you have a game plan and what you'll tackle first the next day. This has made a mega difference in my ability to sleep better at night and knock out a lot in the mornings. By knowing where I'm starting, I don't have to wait for the caffeine to kick in to know what I am doing. I do this for work, my family, and other passion projects that are important to me. I create the list and the space to be able to do what I want and need to while it's top of mind.

Now that we've established that calendars are an effective person's best friend, we can move into how to maximize the 1,440 minutes you've got in your day.

Time Blocks

Next is identifying the amount of time needed to get things done. Cyril Northcote Parkinson wrote an essay for the *Economist* back in 1955 and from there came "Parkinson's Law," which is the adage that work expands to fill the time allotted for its completion.[1] If you give yourself three hours to do a task that should only take 30 minutes, you'll likely use the three hours and lose the time that you could've spent elsewhere. That's why it's essential to evaluate the time needed and block it accordingly.

For example, one of the valuable lessons I learned from my time audit is that I was too giving of the time I spent in my inbox. Once I switched from constantly hitting refresh and responding in the moment to things that could wait, I gained back time and focus. Now, I have dedicated time blocks to clear out the inbox, respond where needed and focus my attention on what needs me most at that moment. I even went as far as to set auto-responses on certain email inboxes that created helpful boundaries and expectations while informing the sender that it could take up to 24–48 business hours for a response. This took some getting used to but it helped me so much. Scheduling the time helped me stay focused on the task at hand and helped me not get distracted by other people's priorities that would distract me from mine.

Additionally, time blocks helped me identify the time of day I was most productive. As I've mentioned, I am far better from a productivity perspective in the morning. I am an early riser and much more efficient in knocking things off the list that require my intellectual capital and creativity. This means that those time

---

[1]https://www.economist.com/news/1955/11/19/parkinsons-law

blocks happen in the morning before lunch. This is also why I only work with clients in the morning; I am not at my best for those interactions later in the day. My afternoon is reserved for the meetings, tasks, or responsibilities that can be effectively accomplished during that time of the day. I also evaluate the week and what else is on my plate so I can assign a realistic amount of time to the task based on what else is going on. I create the boundaries and blocks I need to get what I need to be done in the most efficient way possible because I don't want to waste time on something that could be effectively handled in a shorter, more focused period.

Success Habits

The habits you create are directly connected to the success you will or will not achieve. My mind was blown after reading Brendon Burchard's *High-Performance Habits* many years ago. In fact, his approach and candor were truly the catalysts for my own personal development journey. I knew I was meant for more, and to achieve excellence in my life and career, I wanted a straightforward path to help me identify the areas I needed to improve to fully maximize my potential. Shortly thereafter, I read *Atomic Habits* by James Clear and *Miracle Morning* by Hal Elrod. The motivation and clarity they offered was exactly what I needed to get myself in gear to perform at my best every day. I wasn't the early riser back then, but I knew that if I wanted the "me time" I so desperately needed, I would have to adjust my schedule. Day by day and week by week, I got up a little bit earlier while also going to bed earlier to make up for it. I applied habit stacking, which encourages you to build on what you're already doing to ensure your new habits get adopted early and often. And I was completely open to the feedback from self-assessments that called out that I was not doing enough to take care of myself. I shared in the previous chapter about my morning routine and how I have dedicated time to work on my goals, and that is a direct result of these books. *High-Performance Habits* helped me identify that I needed to take better care of my physical health. *Miracle Morning* helped me rise and shine so I could put myself first, and *Atomic Habits* helped me bake in the workout that needed to happen between my lemon water and coffee.

I now absolutely love my mornings and, over time, have really come to appreciate how much winning the morning makes a difference in my outcomes throughout the day. Sure, every morning won't always be smooth sailing, but the majority of the time, I can step into my day knowing I did what I needed to do for me in order to make progress on the goals I have for myself, and that alone serves as the fuel I need to stay focused on what's next. Whether you're a morning person, a night owl, or a blend of both, really knowing what works best for you is paramount. The busier life gets the more important it is to carve out time for yourself and give yourself the peace of mind to know what you need to get done so that you're not living life in a state of overwhelm or exhaustion. The habits you form and the prioritization of yourself will absolutely change the way in which you show up and what you're able to accomplish. Your habits, good and bad, will absolutely affect you personally and professionally. It could be as simple as creating a routine for yourself to settle into your success habits. I personally love sitting in a comfortable, clean space, with my focus playlist on and relaxing light in the room. This helps me ease into everything else, and I've trained myself to respond positively to these ques and prompts.

Please take stock of what habits you have and whether or not they are serving or sabotaging you. Be honest with yourself. The only way to fix it is to acknowledge it and then create new habits that support the version of you that you want to be.

Stop Multitasking

Every time you introduce an additional element or distraction into your process, you slow down progress and dilute your focus, thus diluting your results.

Every time you introduce an additional element or distraction into your process, you slow down progress and dilute your focus, thus diluting your results. I used to think it was great that I could talk on the phone and draft an email at the same time. It turns out they both suffer. Once I shifted to being present in the moment and showing up with full focus, everything and everyone benefitted. This was exceptionally important with my team. If I was conducting a one-on-one meeting but was also skimming my email, I was not fully focused on them. I could come across as distracted because I was, and that can really rub people the wrong way and make them feel unimportant, which is the last thing I want to do.

I also noticed that this could show up as I was trying to knock out projects on my plate as well. If I allowed conflicting tasks to soak up my energy, I would get less done in the allotted time. Once I shifted to dedicated, focused, and undistracted time blocks, I would actually get way more accomplished in a day than if I allowed myself to multitask. I encourage you to allow yourself to "be" wherever you are and work on whatever needs to be done. Assign the time, and resist the temptation to try to accomplish more than one thing at a time.

Automation = Freedom

We live in a beautiful time where so many aspects of life can be automated. Everything from bill pays to grocery delivery can be automated and free up your time. I am also obsessed with technology and anything that can speed up my ability to get things across the finish line. There are so many incredible tools you can leverage that will give you time back and enable you to focus on where you're needed or what you want to do next. The perfect example of this is content management. When I started my Instagram account during the pandemic, I would create content daily and then schedule an alarm to remind myself to post it. This was ridiculous looking back. I did a quick Google search, and I found amazing tools that would let me preschedule all of my posts, so I didn't even have to think about it. It was a game changer and eliminated what had become a distraction and nagging task on my list every day. I encourage you to think about what can be automated in your life and business. Remember, the goal is freedom of time and returning minutes, even hours, to your days so you can do what you want with them.

Limit Distractions

Please turn it off. In a day and age with countless distractions, it's much more important to put limitations on your ability to be influenced. Social media, Netflix, distracting texts, and unrequested knocks at the door are just a few interruptions or temptations you may face throughout the day. I am encouraging you to protect your time during your golden hours, when you need to work on your priorities and get things done. It can be as simple as muting your phone, putting on noise-canceling headphones, removing notifications on your laptop, or putting a do not disturb sign on your door. These simple steps can completely change the game for you and your time management.

When my husband built his law firm, this became extremely important. He has incredibly well-intentioned people on his team who want to be responsive to their clients, but he was noticing that he was constantly being interrupted and disrupted from doing the work that paid the bills. Thanks to a mentor of his, he established "productivity hours," where he defined blocks during the week that could not be scheduled by others or interrupted unless there was a real emergency. This worked wonders for him and enabled him also to be far more efficient with his follow-up with his team members because he's fully focused on answering their questions once his work is done. I've implemented a similar process and trained my sales leaders to do the same. The natural tendency is to want to check email, respond to social comments, answer someone's question, or take the call, but if it's going to derail you, it's not worth it. It can take you an additional 10–15 minutes to refocus every time you allow a distraction, which will significantly delay your progress. I encourage you to consider what would be helpful for you and make a commitment to communicate what you're doing if necessary and abide by the new boundaries you've put in place.

Avoid Decision Fatigue

If you're looking for a simple approach for better performance overall, this is it. Your brain has a limited capacity to make finite decisions each day, so focusing on the reduction of decisions will help preserve your valuable brain power for other, more important decisions, especially as the day progresses.[2] This may seem simple, but I will tell you, it makes a big difference and will free up your cognitive ability, giving you more mental space and not exhausting your mind. This straightforward concept saves me time and mental space on a daily basis. Because I am tasked with strategic thinking and using my mental capacity throughout the day, I eliminate as many decisions as possible by preplanning.

[2]Hirshleifer, D., Levi, Y., Lourie, B., & Teoh, S. H. (2019). Decision fatigue and heuristic analyst forecasts. *Journal of Financial Economics, 133*(1), 83–98.

This can be as simple as deciding ahead of 6:30 p.m. what we're having for dinner to what I am wearing to work each day that week. And let me tell you, it makes a huge difference. Here are a few things that are preplanned each week at the Walsh household: breakfast, lunch, dinner, wardrobe, who is picking up whom from school, dance, and swimming, to name a few. Peace of mind is a gift, and I appreciate not having to worry about things in the moment. This enables me the time and space to enjoy what I am working on without having to scramble to get things figured out.

Eat the Frog

A common term in the sales world and in others where people struggle with doing the hard things required of them is eating the frog. The saying reminds us to make the moves we need to make versus finding creative ways to avoid them. This can also show up as "getting ready to get ready," only to delay progress and get past what's blocking you. I will 1,000% attest to the fact that the people on my team and the clients that I coach who approach their day with the attitude that the frog will be gone first thing have far better results than those that procrastinate and allow their excuses or anything else to get in their way of making things happen. Next to delaying progress or procrastinating on the tasks that feel harder or bigger than others is the getting ready to get ready time waster. This shows up as stalling, delaying, or constructing other unnecessary roadblocks, all in the vein of delaying what needs to be done. Here are two tips: if it seems big and scary, break it down into bite-size pieces so it's more manageable, and you can tackle it one micro-step at a time. If it's fear that is getting in the way, write down how you will overcome any objections or "failures" you could potentially face. The truth is that you will gain confidence and competence by *doing* what you need to do, and you'll feel so much better once you've crossed it off your list.

And remember, it's better to fail fast and forward, learning from the experience, than to dance around it and delay learning what you need to learn to move through it.

Take Breaks and Know When to Stop

Stop grinding. If you take nothing else from this book, please promise me that it's that simple statement. You will be far less productive if you're grinding, exhausted, stressed, and miserable. Build in times throughout the day that give you the opportunity to recharge. This has been a game changer for me and my team, because we naturally tend to want to put our foot on the gas to get through the day versus pausing to refresh and recharge. Even better, could you plan for it? Going back to the time blocks and calendar, make sure you put these times of restoration on your calendar. It can be as simple as a quick walk, listening or dancing to a few songs you love, or stepping outside for fresh air, but I promise it will make a difference and give you something to look forward to. Plus, you'll be more productive before and after your break rather than forcing yourself to push through. Additionally, knowing when enough is enough will also give you time back. If you notice that you are dragging at the end of the day, take stock of what's draining you and if you can make any helpful shifts when you are tackling those items.

Batch Common Tasks

A quick way to enhance your productivity is to batch similar tasks. Rather than bouncing between a document you're working on and sprinkling calls in between writing the pages, try a call block where you knock out all of those tasks in one swoop. That type of dedicated effort makes you more efficient and less distracted.

Delete and Delegate

If there's someone else that can do the task, delegate it, and if it can be deleted altogether, do so. Do not take on things that don't need to be done by you unless absolutely necessary. This has been such an important lesson for me to learn as I've built companies and my brand. Surrounding myself with competent, trustworthy people who can take things off my plate has changed everything. I try to stay out of the weeds as much as possible and allow people to do what I ask of them. I let go of control and welcomed in support. In my own business alone, it enabled me to grow substantially financially, and at ARS, it enabled me to focus on the revenue engine of the business, which was my team. Look at everything that's on your list and decide how you want to handle that list of responsibilities. Do the calculation of your precious time, meaning how much you make (or could be making) each hour. Compare the value of that task and how much it would cost to have someone else do it. If it makes more financial sense for you to delegate to another person on your team or a virtual assistant, do it. You can generate far more revenue by doing the things only you can do and letting go of the tasks that are weighing you down.

■ ■ ■

I hope this chapter opened your eyes to how much time is available to you daily. If you're reading this book, there's a high likelihood that there are goals and dreams that you want to accomplish, or at least you know that you're capable of amazing things. If finding the time to work on you for you has been difficult, I urge you to try these suggestions. And remember, you don't have to do it all yourself—in fact, you should strive for the opposite. Create the habits you need, embrace the benefits of discipline, and make a commitment to show up today for your future self. Consistency will pay off, and you'll be so proud of what you've been able to accomplish simply by prioritizing what you need and creating the space to make it happen. You deserve it.

9

Build Your Brand
Your Story Is Your Superpower

Whether you have realized this before or not, you have a personal brand. In fact, your brand is the most important one you can and should develop, regardless of your profession. Now, this might be somewhat of a foreign concept to you, and that's totally okay because my intention is that by the end of this chapter, you understand what you need to create or elevate how you're showing up in this world.

Your personal brand is the expertise, experience, and personality that you want everyone else to see. According to the Brand Builder's Group, "it's the digitization and monetization of your reputation." It is the conscious and intentional effort to create and influence public perception by positioning yourself as an authority in your industry, elevating your credibility, and differentiating yourself from the competition to advance your career,

155

increase your circle of influence, and have a larger impact. The experience of building your brand enables you to get crystal clear, create your own lane, and confidently represent the version of yourself that you want others to see.

To set the stage for what's to come, I want you to cleanse your mind from your initial thoughts on branding. And although colors, fonts, and logos play a part in the visual components of branding, we will spend the vast majority of our energy focusing on who you are and how you want to present yourself to the world. I also encourage you to adopt the philosophy that your brand evolves as you do, so you need to commit to your brand's evolution as well and do your best to keep everything up-to-date and in alignment with who you are and how you want to show up.

I can wholeheartedly attest that building my personal brand has unlocked the most incredible opportunities and has inspired me to help so many others do the same. I've spent thousands of hours working with amazing people, helping them to build their brands and package themselves in a way in which they are more marketable; attract incredible, life-changing opportunities; and enhance their confidence tenfold because they know who they are and how they want to represent themselves to the world. In fact, my favorite part of helping my clients build their brands is watching them finally see themselves the way they've always wanted, or for many, they never knew existed. It's a beautiful experience, and it forever changes the way they show up in person and online. That newfound confidence gives them clarity and direction and opens their eyes to the unlimited opportunities that they can pursue.

On top of the confidence gained from investing and developing your brand, the data backs up how critical it is to take this seriously, especially when you're focused on growing your business or customer base. Brand Builder's Group released a national study in 2022[1] highlighting the impact of brand building on one's ability to grow their business and influence. The consistent through line regardless of generation, was that people with recognizable personal brands benefited tremendously. In fact, 74% of Americans were more likely to trust an individual and 63% were more inclined to buy from or do business with someone who has a personal brand versus someone who does not. These statistics further reinforce that doing the work on your brand will pay off regardless of your profession, and I am excited to share more about how and why as we do a deep dive into your personal brand.

Expertise, Authority, and Trust

Your brand should focus on building your expertise, authority, and trust, enhancing your presence, and elevating your credibility. Bolstering your expertise in a truthful manner will help make you the go-to expert in your industry, and enhancing

The more people trust you, the more likely they will buy from you, hire you, or want to do business with you.

your visibility will attract more clients, customers, and contracts. When it comes to your authority, being a thought leader in your space will give you additional opportunities to be viewed and turned to and will elevate your presence in your industry. Last, the trust factor is paramount and is what branding experts today consider to be one of the most important aspects of building your brand. The more people trust you, the more likely they will buy from you, hire you, or want to do business with you. Ultimately, the more you focus on your expertise, authority, and trust, the greater the likelihood that your brand will exhibit the

[1]Brand Builders. The future of business is here. https://brandbuildersgroup.com/study/

trust-building elements that will enhance your profitability and possibilities.

I'm so excited to share with you many valuable frameworks and lessons I've taught over the years. This chapter is broken down into several sections to help you identify who you are, how you want to show up, who you're trying to attract and serve, and what you want the results to look like by investing in your personal brand. This will work; I've seen it be applicable for many individuals regardless of their profession or career stage.

Know Who You're Trying to Attract and What You Hope to Gain

To kick this off, we need to be really clear about what you're trying to accomplish by building your brand. Are you trying to earn more opportunities in your workplace? Are you trying to monetize your influence online? Do you want speaking opportunities or a book deal? Are you thinking about launching your own business or side hustle? There are countless reasons that could be your motivating factor, but no matter what, you owe it to yourself to do this work because you will become more aware of the possibilities by spending time on your brand.

Back in my early twenties, I was a passionate advocate for mental health and would share my story with anyone who would listen. Over a few short years, I had built my reputation and brand, and so many doors opened because I was visible and showed up consistently sharing my story. Those opportunities turned into paid brand deals and jobs, and eventually, my ability to do this for myself evolved into high-paying opportunities to help others do it, too. Regardless of what's on the immediate horizon or even farther out in the future, starting on, refining, and committing to your personal brand development will eventually increase your earning potential and help you stay on the radar of those who need what you have. You can't hide under a rock and pray that people find you. You have to actively share who you are, why you're the go-to person, and build trust with those you're trying to attract through thoughtful and intentional actions that unlock your potential.

When it comes to the who, you must clearly define your ideal customers, clients, or audiences. It's not uncommon to have a couple of different personas that you need to focus your energy and attention on. Remember, your brand is important not only for you personally but also it's incredibly important that it's aligned professionally if you're looking to monetize it or make more money as a result of enhancing your visibility or brand awareness. I highly recommend that you spend the time, energy, and effort needed to map out who you want to serve. I've included exercises at www.shebelievedbook.com/resources that will help you, and I encourage you to go through the process for the various customers or clients you want more of. Using the Venn diagram in Figure 9.1 will help you tremendously as you define your

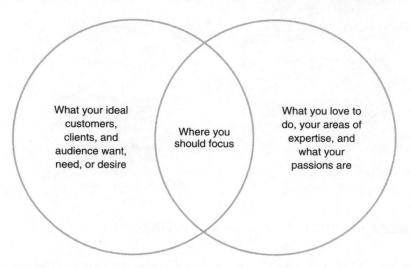

FIGURE 9.1 A Venn diagram to help you define your message.

messaging and create the content pillars, meaning the core topics you're going to consistently discuss, that will enable you to build your expertise and offer value to your customers and keep you from getting overwhelmed in the process and focused on the most important areas of your brand.

The Four Ms of Personal Branding

The brand-building framework I created and have relied on for the last decade makes it easier to break down the process and areas of focus that will help you package and present your brand. I call these areas the four Ms, which also makes them easy to remember. Figure 9.2 provides an overview of the framework.

Brand Building Framework

01	MINDSET	Develop confidence and clarity in why your brand is important and how you want to represent yourself.
02	MESSAGING	Define your messaging so it can be clear, cohesive, and consistent to attract the right clients, customers, and accounts.
03	MARKETING	Develop a strategy to get your brand in front of the right people.
04	MONETIZATION	Maximize your ability to generate revenue thanks to the expertise, authority, and trust you've established with your brand.

(c) Allison Walsh Consulting

FIGURE 9.2   The four Ms of personal brand building.

Mindset

Because everything starts with your belief system, mindset is the first *M* we will focus on.

Everything starts with your belief system and mindset.

As we've discussed throughout this book, what we believe about ourselves significantly affects how we show up. When I start working with my clients, we do a deep dive into the limiting beliefs and their fears about showing up and work through any challenges they've had in the past when it comes to going after what they want. A common theme is that they're willing to do the work, but as it gets closer to their brand launch, they can get fearful of what other people may think about them becoming intentionally more visible. I encourage them to stop spending energy on other people's opinions and focus on what increasing their reach means in relation to the impact they will have or the results they will achieve by showing up in a more cohesive and consistent manner. I'm always there to assure them that this is the best next move, and once they've got some time under their belts and positive results because of their brand exposure, it makes it that much easier to shine the spotlight even brighter. Just like everything else regarding confidence, the more you practice it, the easier it becomes. When you lean into your uniqueness and allow yourself to authentically and genuinely show up, you create unbelievable opportunities for yourself and those you serve. Remember that no one is you, and that is your superpower.

Remember that no one is you, and that is your superpower.

Embrace who *you* are because the world needs you and your gifts and talents. Do not be intimidated by others who are farther along in their journeys than you are now. They all had a day one, too, and with consistency and intention they are where they are today because they kept putting one foot in front of the next. Release the additional pressure that you may be applying to be perfect right out of the gate. That's unrealistic, and those types of expectations end up stealing your joy and increasing your stress. Instead, focus on daily progress, being 1% better like we've discussed before, and surrounding yourself with those who can help you get where you want to go.

Messaging

The second *M* in the brand-building framework is messaging. Included in this section are the content and the way in which you want to package your brand, so for those who enjoy the aesthetic elements of brand building, you'll love this area. Out of the four Ms, this area does require a lot of behind-the-scenes work, but it is what enables numbers three and four in the framework to do what they need to do, so it is time well spent.

Included in the framework's messaging section is all the content you want to share about yourself and how you want to package it. This includes but is not limited to your bio, résumé, content related to your expertise, and the way in which you want to present your brand. My clients love this area because we give them clear brand guidelines, also known as their guard rails, to help them stay consistent, clear, and cohesive. This is where we define your core themes, or content pillars, that you will focus on to make sure you are not diluting your message or confusing those whom you're trying to attract, but even more, it will help you stay on brand and on message at all times. When defining your content pillars, these should be areas that make sense for you to be talking about while also enabling you to build your expertise, authority, and trust.

Now you might be wondering where to even begin, and I'm going to ask you now to put a pen to paper as we go through the beginning stages and phases of defining who you are and why you're amazing, and it all begins with *you*. In *Platform: The Art and Science of Personal Branding*,[2] Cynthia Johnson, who also happens to be a wonderful friend and advisor, beautifully articulates four areas in which one should focus their attention while building their brands:

1. **Personal proof:** your education, experience, and certifications

2. **Social proof:** includes guest blogging, speaking engagements, testimonials, references, media mentions, and interviews, and so on

3. **Association:** includes companies and people you work with, volunteer for, or associate with; essentially, you are whom you hang out with and whom you associate with

4. **Recognition:** top lists, competitions, awards, and acknowledgments received

By listing everything out, you can more easily identify where you might need to spend more time developing an area or you might even notice an area that you didn't even realize was so impressive. This audit will help you in the immediate future to lean on what's been accomplished and give you areas that you can focus on, or perhaps a new goal to strive for, as you continue to build your brand.

You need to decide what you want to be known for and what topics you want to lend your expertise to. I encourage you to start with no more than five content pillars, and please reflect on your Venn diagram to ensure that there is overlap with those you're trying to attract. Remember, we are intentionally trying to build your expertise, authority, and trust with every post, newsletter, blog, column, speaking engagement, and media

[2]Johnson, C. (2019). Platform: The art and science of personal branding. Potter/TenSpeed/Harmony/Rodale.

opportunity, so alignment is important if you're trying to maximize your investment of time and energy and not confuse those you're trying to attract.

For example, these are the areas that I focus on:

- Personal brand building
- Personal and professional development
- Success strategies
- Mindset and confidence
- Mental health and wellness

These five pillars enable me to produce clear content that my audience, clients, and customers want and need. When I work on keynotes, articles, or social content, I use these as my guiding light because I know, thanks to defining my ideal clients and customers, that they need what I have to offer. I understand their pain points and can focus on producing quality content that serves their needs. This approach also makes it more about them and less about me, which also assists in making my brand more approachable and appealing.

I encourage you to list all the things you could be speaking about or creating content about and look at the overlapping areas of need that your customers or clients have. The sweet spot is in the overlap and where you should spend the majority of your time.

I also encourage you to humanize your message as much as possible and appropriately. Whether you are focused on business-to-business or business-to-customer, it's all human-to-human. Give yourself the chance to show up as an authentic, multidimensional, real person because you will be more relatable and, chances are, earn the trust of those you're trying to attract much quicker than if you did not. Gone are the days when everything has to be picture-perfect. It's far more important to be visible, authentic, and aligned with your core pillars than worry about perfectly constructed messaging and imagery.

Your Story Is Your Superpower: Four Ps to Pitch Yourself Perfectly

One of the most important things you can do, whether you're working for yourself or someone else, or simply want to be able to stand up and share who you are with confidence and grace, is to master your message.

This chapter includes my go-to framework for pitching yourself with ease. This has literally been used thousands of times and is tried and true. Everything from boardrooms to the Miss America stage, this framework will give you the confidence to own whatever room, interview, microphone, or stage that you are on or in.

What I love most about this is that it's like an accordion. It can be as straightforward and simple as a few sentences or can be expanded on if you've got more time to go into further detail. I've used it to train salespeople, authors, speakers, experts, and thousands of ambitious individuals who just want more confidence when someone says, "Tell me about yourself." It's also easily adaptable, meaning that you can flex your messaging based on whom you're speaking to at that time. As we discussed, you may have a few ideal clients or personas that you are trying to resonate with. This formula will enable you to tailor your talking points to meet their needs.

- **Passion.** We open the framework with a brief introduction of yourself. Keep it short and sweet because most people are initially subliminally seeking a connection point to something that they care about as they listen, so we want to get to the second *P* as soon as possible.

- **Purpose.** This step in the framework is about *them*. We want to pique their interest or help them realize how important what you do, sell, or provide is. This is also a great place to insert a stat to demonstrate the greater need or impact. Don't be shy here, and remember that numbers are memorable. I encourage you to use one impressive or eye-opening stat in this section to hook the listener.

- **Proof.** This is where you will demonstrate your unique expertise, authority, and credibility. Feel free to sprinkle in notable honors, experience, or other credibility boosters that accentuate you and your trust factor. Don't be shy!

- **Plan.** This is your segue to how you will help them or propel your work forward. Remember to focus on them, what problems you're going to solve or promises you're willing to make to help them reach their goals.

Figure 9.3 provides you with a template to capture all of this.

CUSTOMER/CLIENT/AUDIENCE: _____

PASSION	**PURPOSE**
Who are you and why do you care?	*Why should they care?*

PROOF	**PLAN**
What have you done?	*What do you plan to do?*

FIGURE 9.3 Four Ps to develop your pitch.

Let's Get Visual

I encourage you to create the aesthetic elements that best represent you and your brand while keeping your audience in mind. There are amazing tools like Canva that can help you, and I've included them at www.shebelievedbook.com/resources. Leaning on these types of platforms will make your life so much easier and enable you to easily stay on brand as you're creating the digital and visual assets that will help you put your best foot forward. I use Canva for literally everything—from my social posts to workbooks, résumés, and marketing materials. You can create and save your brand tools to help you quickly and consistently create what you need forward-facing to show up as your best.

Invest in a good headshot or brand photography. Take advantage of the fact that it's not hard to get a great photo of yourself these days. Even if you're not ready to invest in a professional headshot or brand shoot (which I do recommend), phones are incredibly powerful and can capture what you need. If you are going to work with a photographer, pick one who is well-suited for you and has experience with the type of shoot you're looking for.

If you are investing in a brand shoot, which often includes multiple looks, I recommend creating a mood or inspiration board composed of photos that you would like to emulate before your shoot and share it with your photographer. This is an investment, and these photos will be extremely valuable for you as you continue to put yourself out there. I use Pinterest for motivation and inspiration and create my mood boards in Canva as well.

There are many dos and don'ts when it comes to photoshoots, and I've included a helpful checklist at www.shebelievedbook.com/resources for you to reference if this is something you want to do. Once you have a great headshot, use it everywhere. The more people see it, the more people will recognize you and

your photo. It should be your profile photo on all social platforms, on your website if you have one, and you can even include
it on the signature line in your email address. A professional
photo elevates your digital presence and gives you the confidence
to know you're representing yourself well.

Audit

Just as important as intentionally focusing on what you share
with the world is auditing what already exists. Your history is
only a Google search away, and the messages you're sending
could not be on brand with the version of yourself that you'd like
to represent. I have not hired dozens of job candidates over the
course of my career based on a digital footprint that was not in
alignment with our brand standards, and I know I am not alone.
Colleges and universities do it as well, and so does the media. You
must be mindful of what you post, share, and comment on
because it can and will be resurfaced at inopportune times. Your
digital footprint is your reputation and responsibility. Guard it,
protect it, and certainly don't compromise it. I highly recommend setting up a Google alert on your name, so you're always
notified when it's mentioned. This will help you stay aware of
what's out there and be able to handle or respond accordingly.
But, even more important, think before you post and always be
mindful of the company you keep.

Marketing

The third *M* revolves around the way in which you are going to
market yourself and how. This includes all the places and spaces
where you're promoting who you are and what you do, inclusive
of in person, in print, and online. This could include various
social channels, your website, any tangible marketing materials,

events, conferences, media, speaking opportunities, books, and the list goes on and on. You must focus on where your ideal clients are so you're showing up in the right places, not just where you want to be showing up. Once again, the three Cs—clear, consistent, and cohesive—should lead the way and will help make it easier for people to understand what you do and say yes. Please ensure that you're looking at all your marketing materials in totality and be open to regular revisions as you evolve. When you invest in your brand, you'll have the confidence to show up knowing you're ready for what's next, but it also takes courage to do so. Remember that if you don't share who you are and what you do with the world, they won't know, and it would be a disservice to not share your gifts.

In addition to all of the self-generated marketing materials and opportunities that you should be focused on, I cannot stress enough how valuable it is to get on other stages. By this, I mean getting in front of other people's audiences and customer bases that include ideal clients and customers for you, too. This could be as simple as being on someone's podcast or contributing an article to a magazine to as significant as formal collaborations, partnerships, or joint ventures. Again, alignment is paramount, and you should always evaluate if there's potential for you within the offers you receive or the avenues you're pursuing. The more visible you are and the more buzz you create, the more opportunities will be available to you. Remember that not all of them will align with your goals, and it's totally okay to say no. Also, be mindful of who you affiliate with, because that can either be a credibility booster or detractor from the beautiful brand that you've created.

Please note that marketing costs can accumulate quickly if you're not mindful, so consider how much you're willing to spend on your brand. If you're a business owner, you can build this into your marketing budget, but if you're a solopreneur or building your brand on your own dime, I would encourage you to create a budget that you're willing to dedicate to this effort. Once you have established your budget, then you can identify vendors or professionals who will help you remain within your financial parameters. It's important to focus on what you want the return on your investment to be before you spend money, but don't be penny wise and pound foolish. It's a noisy market, and you have to consistently show up and do the proper follow-up when you're marketing yourself. As a rule of thumb, a potential customer or client would need to be exposed to your brand eight times before making a buying decision. That means that it's even more important for you to think of all of the ways you can be and places you should be to introduce your brand and what you offer to those you want to serve. This mentality shouldn't be just for entrepreneurs or those trying to purely monetize their personal brands. This goes for those trying to establish themselves within their own organizations or potentially move to other companies.

Trust in the preparation you will have done to thoughtfully build your brand from the first two Ms we discussed because, naturally, there can be some hesitation when it comes to actually promoting yourself. Countless clients of mine throughout the years have really had to lean on the mindset work we did, in the beginning, to be able to hit post, send, and publish on their various marketing materials. But because their messaging and branding were spot on and truly reflected how they wanted to represent themselves, they could trust that they were sending the right message to the world.

You can, too, and my hope is that you take the time to map out the various places and spaces you should be showing up. Come up with a targeted list that your ideal customers or clients pay attention to or allow to influence them. Some of these examples may be social channels, podcasts, websites, shows, conferences, networking groups, or associations. Once you have your list, identify contact information, and start reaching out to see if you can participate, post, be a guest or speaker, or offer your expertise. Always present the value you can add and how it will help them when pitching yourself. Although you may get a few rejections along the way, I encourage you to keep asking because one yes can make a major difference and open additional doors. Just like with everything else we've discussed, create goals for building your brand because, regardless of your profession, title, or career, your brand is one of the most valuable assets that you can leverage.

Monetization

The beautiful upside to spending the time on the first three Ms is if it's done well, your opportunities to monetize significantly increase. Whether your goal is to earn more financially within your current organization, be recognized as a top candidate for a new opportunity, create your own company, or get paid directly as an influencer or brand ambassador, personal branding can help you achieve all of those objectives. And although I've been focused on building my brand for over two decades, in the past year alone, the work I've done expanding on those efforts opened doors for me to write this book, speak on international stages, collaborate with incredible people, and secure lucrative brand deals with businesses I love. Now, this didn't happen overnight, but it did happen because of ultra-focused efforts to get my brand in front of the right people and, most important, asking for the business. I kept showing up, tracking my progress, setting intentional brand expansion goals, and I didn't get discouraged if something didn't work out because there are abundant opportunities out there if you're willing to do the work.

We now live in what I refer to as a creators' economy, and it's relatively easy to monetize your own brand and content these days. One example is Instagram. I wasn't active on the platform until the pandemic. I saw an opportunity for me to lean in, but it required me to be consistent and intentional. It became an incredibly valuable marketing tool for me, and I was attracting ideal clients that I was so excited to work with. From there, it became a tool to monetize through Instagram's campaigns, which evolved into five-figure brand deals and collaborations. Publishers even reached out via Instagram to see if I was interested in writing a book. Simply showing up daily, serving up valuable content to my audience, and being clear about whom I serve opened so many doors for me, and this type of intentional effort can do the same for you, too.

Putting It All Together

To help you drill down and focus on each area, I've included a list of questions to prompt you to think about your own brand. I can't stress enough how valuable it is to spend time on this now and as you evolve personally and professionally. Whether your goal is to package yourself and enhance your confidence or if you're looking to monetize it as a stand-alone revenue driver, it's worth the time and energy.

Mindset
- What do you want to be known for?
- How do you want to be perceived?
- Who is your ideal client/audience that you're trying to reach/attract?
- What fears do you have when you think about sharing more about yourself with the world?
- Has anything held you back in the past?

Messaging

- How do you articulate who you are and what you do?
- How do you want to visually come across in person and online?
- What's your proof?
- What does your digital footprint say about you now?
- How do you *want* to describe your brand versus how it is now?

Marketing

- Where do you need to show up to boost your visibility and brand recognition?
- Who are the top 10 experts in your space, and how can you connect with them?
- What networking groups/associations do you need to be a part of?
- Where are your ideal clients, and how can you connect with them?

Monetization

- How can you monetize your brand?
- What value do you have, and how can you align your brand with strategic opportunities?
- What financial goals do you have when it comes to your brand?

As I am sure you can tell, I am a firm believer in the value of investing in your brand. It can truly transform your life, opportunities, and, most important, your confidence. You deserve abundant success and the world needs what you have to offer, which is why it's critically important to do the work to show up, shine bright, and lean into your brand. Do the work now to expand your brand and access your next level of success, because if you don't share with the world what you do, they won't know about the special gifts and talents you have. I promise you, you'll be so grateful that you did and your future self will be well positioned for the possibilities that will head your way. It's time to turn your spotlight on full beam and celebrate the unique person you are. Shine bright because the world needs what you have. You are more amazing than you give yourself credit for, and you deserve all of the abundance available to you because of your willingness to share your gifts with the world. Build your brand. It will be 1,000% worth it.

10

Embrace Your Evolution
When to Lean into New Opportunities

Have you ever had a feeling that something wasn't right? Deep down inside you knew something was off but couldn't quite put your finger on it? I sure have, and this feeling surfaced most recently at a time that I didn't expect.

When I began working on this book, I felt unsettled whenever I looked at the last chapter. Something wasn't right. However, I kept ignoring that there was a significant change that needed to take place. After all, I had worked extremely hard to be at the point where I was and there were many amazing things to look forward to. I had been a valued member of the Advanced Recovery Systems (ARS) team for nearly 10 years and had simultaneously built a lucrative and fulfilling business. And, thanks to the work I had done on my personal brand, I had amazing opportunities to work with incredible clients, speak on stages around the world and increase my impact through various brand campaigns and collaborations. Why on earth would I want to change any of that?!?

I will forever be grateful for the opportunity to put all of these words on paper and share my heart with you. During this experience, I was able to really look in the mirror and evaluate if I was living my truth, and with every page written and chapter completed, I realized the answer was no. So much of my identity was tied to something I had built. I had to learn to disconnect, let myself be me, and be really honest about what was going on.

The reason the original last chapter wasn't feeling the way it should was that it wasn't the chapter that deep down I wanted to write. Rather, I needed a life overhaul more than I realized, and I became committed to doing what I needed to do to be able to write this chapter from a place of integrity while staying aligned with my truth. Most important, if I was going to share all of this advice and encouragement with you to live boldly and optimize your own potential, it was critically important for me to be doing the same thing.

I had always heard that writing a book was an incredibly therapeutic process, but I had no idea what an emotional and liberating one it would be. And, in my case, the timing could not have been more perfect. I preach living in alignment with yourself and creating the life you want, but I know that it's important to allow your momentum to carry you to higher levels that may require you to make very difficult and oftentimes unexpected changes. And when opportunities come knocking and your calling is pulling you in a different direction, it's paramount that you tune into yourself and answer the call.

My love for ARS runs deep. I take tremendous pride in what we've built and the tens of thousands of lives we've saved. Over the course of my career at ARS, my reasons for being involved continued to deepen as loved ones were affected, some even losing their battles. I was on a mission to create access to care so we could get people well rather than having to say goodbye. Most important, I absolutely adore the team I put together, trained, and poured into for the last decade. While I entered the behavioral health industry because I had a passion to help others, my team had very much become my why during my leadership career. All that being said, mid-2021 was a cause to pause. As I shared earlier, I was experiencing burnout and challenges we had never planned for. In addition, a few triggering situations happened, and I needed some real support to help me process what I was experiencing. I felt my spirit weaken, losing the fight within myself to fully show up and shine bright the way I encourage everyone else to do. I always say that your energy introduces you even before you speak, and I could no longer manufacture the energy to hide that deep down inside that I knew I had outgrown my current situation, and my comfort zone had become a crutch to keep me playing small.

I couldn't understand what was really going on until almost a year later. The truth that I didn't want to accept was that I had maxed out in my position, and I was staring straight into the eyes of no upward mobility, which didn't sit well with me at all. Complacency is a terrible feeling for me and my team was very familiar with my common reminder that "complacency is where dreams go to die." While I continued to invest in and surround myself with amazing people to help me develop my skill sets and opportunities for my own brand and business, the same type of evolution was not unfolding at ARS. I kept going, day in and day out, hoping it would change. But, the more momentum I gained externally, the more difficult it became internally. I felt stuck in a past version of myself that I had outgrown, and despite showing up every day with a smile on my face and the intention and ability to make a difference, those closest to me sensed my spirit weakening. At the core of all my hesitations was this: why on earth would I compromise or sacrifice the decade-long commitment to building a company that I cared so deeply about to exit at this stage? After all, I had dreamed of creating a mission-driven "unicorn company," meaning one valued at $1 billion, that was changing the game while simultaneously affecting the lives of thousands of people every year that we were in operation. We were so close.

My Achilles' heel is that I can be loyal to a fault, and the thought of letting go was not appealing when I had so many close relationships and people I loved at ARS. It was also difficult for me to wrap my head around leaving before we sold. I had come up with a million reasons and excuses not to quit, even though my soul was not on fire like it once had been. It was going to take something pretty spectacular to lure me away and a big flashing sign from the universe to get me to make a move. Thankfully for my stubborn self, I got both.

I'll never forget July 2022. I had recently completed the roll-out of a new training program at ARS that leveraged the amazing tools from the positive psychology coach certification program I had been a part of earlier that year. The feedback was incredible and many employees were crediting their retention as a result of what they had gained. I, alongside the training director for the department, had poured into the team and I spent a lot of time focusing on strengths-based coaching to help elevate their mindsets, confidence, well-being, and performance.

During this entire 10-week experience, I kept reflecting on if I was truly in a position to use my strengths to the best of my ability, or if I had passively cosigned on my existence and my role at ARS. It was also incredibly important to me to constantly feel like I was growing and leveling up in my position, and the reality was that I was not. I had reached my peak, and there were no indications, despite multiple conversations and meetings with leadership, that anything was going to change. In fact, I made it a point to ask every week for three months following the completion of that training program and the answer remained the same. That experience was the eye-opener that I needed to realize that something had to change if I wanted to continue to evolve in the way that I always encourage others to do as well. And because God and the Universe work in unbelievable ways, there were multiple opportunities hitting my LinkedIn inbox and cell phone at this time. In years past, I declined the calls and politely rejected the requests to meet with companies. And in all honesty, I hadn't really even entertained the thought of staying in the industry. I had grown my own business substantially and had exciting projects and opportunities available that would allow me to work less and earn more. I always assumed that once we sold ARS, I would double down on my own business and never look back.

And then on July 25, a message popped into my inbox from an ambitious, driven, well-respected founder named Carter Barnhart that caused me to reconsider my position. She was requesting time from me, and this time, I obliged. I initially offered up time as an advisory board member or a limited consulting agreement, but with each additional conversation and discussion, I became more and more intrigued with her fast-growing, life-changing company. I saw how I could help this new start-up reach higher levels, and I felt incredibly respected for what I was bringing to the table. I was lit up about what I could help her build, leveraging the experience and lessons learned the hard way over the years. There was something magical about her and the vision of the company that got me excited about getting involved in yet another start-up all over again. Plus, the focus of her company, Charlie Health, was adolescent and young adult mental health, a cause near and dear to my heart.

As the weeks went by and I continued to advance through the process, I knew this was going to be an experience that warranted my board of advisors. It was also important that I take my time and not make an emotional decision or one rooted in disappointment or resentment. I had to be 1,000% at peace in order to take the plunge.

I am now going to share with you the process that I went through as I evaluated whether or not this was the right move for me, and I encourage you to think about yourself as I go through each section and consider how this applies to you. Even if you're completely happy with what you're doing right now, I want you to reflect on whether or not there are opportunities to enhance your day-to-day experience in your current role, position, company, or even your own business. And, of course, if you've got a calling to do something different and actualize your potential in even bigger ways either through a career change, starting a side hustle, or jumping into entrepreneurship, this will help. Ultimately, I want you to truly evaluate where you are versus where you want to be and be honest with yourself about your own alignment. If you're not headed straight toward your next level, this will be very beneficial for you and will help surface where there are opportunities for you as well.

Get Clarity

First, I had to really think about what I wanted in this next stage and phase of life. What on my current list of roles and responsibilities did I want to keep? What did I want to get rid of? What lit me up and brought me joy? What was I really good at? What depleted me versus fulfilled me? What enabled me to tap into the strengths I have and leverage them in a meaningful way? Making a list of all of those answers helped me extract my key areas of focus, and, most important, create my list for an ideal role or consulting opportunity. It was important to me as I entertained this position and others during this time that I wasn't wearing rose-colored glasses, only choosing to see the areas that appealed to me. I wanted to ensure that this would enable me to leverage my experience, while also affording me the chance to stretch, grow, and evolve. The last thing I wanted was to take a step backward or not feel intellectually stimulated. The chance to make an impact at scale while being connected to a mission-driven organization were also two areas that I didn't want to ignore, because deep down I know my motivation stems from creating change in a positive way both for those I am leading and those our company is serving. After evaluating this particular opportunity, as well as a few others that had made their way to me during this time of contemplation, I felt confident that I could check all of the boxes and should keep the process going.

I also needed to get super clear about what I wanted life to look like over the next several months and years. Just because I could do it and do it well, doesn't necessarily mean I should. I needed to be really honest with myself about what I was willing to do at this stage in my life knowing full well that whenever there is change, it takes a greater investment in oneself to get acclimated, up-to-date, and achieve goals. I continued to evaluate what I would need to say no to if I decided to say yes to this opportunity. I didn't want to resent what this would pull me away from and I needed to be at peace with the discomfort of not knowing everything I needed to know right out of the gate. After all, I had invested a lot of time, energy, and attention into laying the groundwork for post-ARS life in my own business and this unexpected plot twist wasn't something that I had considered.

It was also important to prioritize the most important humans in my life and how I needed to show up for them. One of the things that the COVID-19 pandemic spotlighted for me was how much I enjoyed being home, even if it was a bit chaotic, and I wanted to be more present for my kids and husband. This new opportunity would enable me to be based from my home office and contain my travel to once a month. I really appreciated that and what that would do for our family.

If you're potentially considering a new opportunity, I encourage you to ask yourself these questions to help you gain clarity:

- If I say yes to a new opportunity, whom and what am I saying no to?
- Would a new opportunity enable me to create the work-life integration to support the people in my life who are my priority?
- What do I want to continue doing outside of work and does this allow me the time and space to do that?

In addition to clarity on the logistics, I also focused on what this would need to look like financially. After all, I would be walking away from a substantial package at ARS and would likely modify my own business for the first several months as I got acclimated to a new company. I also have three kids, and two of them are competitive dancers, so there's no shortage of financial responsibilities around here. I was not interested in taking a step backward and wanted the opportunity to earn more in the long run, so I needed to be crystal clear about the financial aspect as I engaged in conversations.

I sat down with my spreadsheet and created multiple scenarios to determine what the new number would need to look like in order for me to make a move. I also had to evaluate what I was walking away from, as I had given nearly 10 years of my life to an organization and had a stake in the game that would easily disappear as a result of my departure. This was one of the hardest decisions because I had been looking forward to the financial gains of a sale process and had certainly poured my heart and soul into building the company from scratch.

If there is an opportunity that you'd like to pursue, take the time to gain clarity in the financial impact of your decisions. Financial questions to help you include the following:

- What is the ideal financial target that enables you to feel financially secure and appreciated for the value you bring to the table?

- What are the current salaries or consulting fees available for similar positions?

- Would this be more beneficial as a consulting position, or should you go all in as a full-time team member?

- What additional benefits need to be available for you to make a move?

Last, I had to get clear about how I needed and wanted to feel in my new role. It was critically important that there was chemistry between myself and those whom I would be working closely with. I wanted to be led the way I like to lead, and I was adamant that I would be in a positive environment with driven people who respected one another. I love creating positive emotional experiences for my people and it was clear this founder did as well.

As you consider what kind of culture is the best fit for your personality and ideal career trajectory, ask questions like these:

- What is the culture like?
- What is the workplace dynamic?
- How do you take care of your people?
- Provide examples of how you support one another in a remote environment.
- Is there an opportunity to meet with someone who is already on the team and successful in this or a similar role?

And last, I needed to future cast, meaning consider how this opportunity, if accepted, would enable me to actualize and optimize my own potential. It was also important to evaluate if it would limit me in ways that were unacceptable at this stage and phase of my life and career. I needed to be able to see growth for at least three years and thankfully, for this ambitious start-up, that was crystal clear.

Do the Internal Work

There were a lot of emotions that surfaced as I started to get serious about making a move. After a few too many heart-wrenching days, I enlisted the help of an amazing therapist and coach to help me really sort through what I was feeling. It was important to me that I did not make an emotional decision and that I was completely at peace. She helped me unpack the feelings and emotions I had been carrying, enabling me to create the closure I needed to make this significant decision.

I also was fiercely committed to my daily practice of meditation, gratitude, and exercise. I made it a point to sit down and write out all of the things I was grateful for over the last 10 years so I could allow myself to channel my energy in a positive direction and honor the experience in a meaningful way. I added in additional walks around the block and "less noise," meaning I wasn't always listening to a book or podcast like usual. I allowed myself to think the thoughts and feel the feelings. I do believe that God and the Universe send signs and it's difficult to notice them if you are constantly distracted. As time went on, these became more and more apparent and gave me additional confidence that I was headed in the right direction.

It was also important for me to recognize and address any distorted thoughts. It's easy to feel overwhelmed and powerless in the face of life's challenges—our brains are wired to create mental filters that can leave us feeling deflated or anxious. But with awareness, we have the power to recognize these cognitive distortions as they arise and make choices that empower rather than limit us. Cognitive distortions are negative thought patterns that aren't based on reality or facts, and changing these patterns will help your overall mental well-being.[1] Thanks to the training I received from positive psychology and the course we put together for the team, I was flush with great resources to help identify when these very natural, but sometimes extremely challenging, thoughts can creep in. Some examples of this are all or nothing thinking, catastrophizing, or leaning on should, meaning, I should have done this or that.

Because this was a huge, and in some ways, a very scary decision for me, I had to stop the negative thoughts in their tracks. It was really easy for me to think of all of the ways this wouldn't work rather than leaning into all of the clear indicators that it would. A dear friend reminded me, as did this dynamic founder during the interview process, that it very well could work out even better than I could imagine. I embraced that mindset and leaned into the possibilities of the future.

Be Prepared for Challenges That Test Your Commitment

When I look back at some of the most pivotal moments in my life, they've also been accompanied by a significant challenge that simultaneously transpired and truly put me and my decision to go for it to the test. I do believe that these situations percolate to test our commitment to our desires, and this decision was no different. Just like the crazy test of commitment I experienced

---

[1]Joy, R. (2022 October 25). What are cognitive distortions and how can you change these thinking patterns? *Healthline*. https://www.healthline.com/health/cognitive-distortions

back in 2006 when I was simultaneously dealing with a breakup and food poisoning during the Miss Florida week, this life-changing decision came with unexpected challenges as well.

Three months to the day of the initial conversation with Carter and having gone through a dozen or so more meetings and discussions, the ink was dry on the contract and I was preparing to have the impending conversation with leadership at ARS. I had decided that November 1 would be the day I gave notice of my exit and departure so I would have ample time to wrap up before my intended start date. Well, on Halloween, our worlds were rocked in the Walsh household when one of children started experiencing pain, swelling all over their body, and excruciating headaches. What we had hoped would be a quick visit to the doctor to get answers and relief turned into the need to rush to the children's hospital. They were admitted nearly immediately as their blood pressure was dangerously high and the lab work was all out of whack.

Talk about being an emotional basket case. Not only were we struggling with the stress of not knowing what was happening, but I was about to make a *major* move that already had me a bit anxious as I did not know how the news would be received. Regardless, I knew that I had to keep leaning forward.

I will forever remember sitting on the park bench in front of the hospital, making the phone call that would change not only my life but many others affected by the ripple effect of this decision. I was extremely aware that this news would catch many off guard and I wanted to handle it appropriately. Thankfully, it was received better than anticipated, and we made a plan for what to do next. As I shared the news with my team and colleagues, no one was surprised as to my why. It was continuously reflected back to me that I had always pushed them to be 1% better each and every day, to live outside of their comfort zones, and to chase bold and big dreams. During many conversations, the commentary was actually "I'm surprised it took this long," and they were right, but I had to be ready and I also believe that timing is everything when it comes to aligning with life-changing opportunities.

As I've mentioned before, my love for each of them was a driving force for why I stayed so long, and I was committed to spending the final days and time available with anyone who needed or wanted it. I opened up my calendar and scheduled more than 30 one-on-one sessions, which filled my cup while I poured into them during our last coaching and mentoring sessions. It was during those conversations that I truly realized the growth that so many of them had experienced, and I will forever cherish the kind words shared with me as we wrapped up our time together. It was important to me that I radiated gratitude and appreciation in every conversation. I wanted each team member to know that I was thankful for them, our relationship, and their contribution to the success of the organization. My biggest concerns revolved around ensuring that the groundwork that was laid would continue and that each of them would be taken care of and continuously empowered to strive for more, achieve their goals, and level up regardless of time or tenure on the team. I worked with the leadership team to connect them with coaches and trainers, and game plans were created to support the team through this transition and beyond.

Those final days were a powerful reminder that we are creating a legacy each and every day. The way we treat people makes a massive difference, and living your truth is one of the most important things you can do despite the challenging feat that it is. It was also apparent that I had to be grounded in my decision in order to handle the dozens of conversations that resulted from my ripping off the bandage. And, most important, I had to remind myself that I was doing this for me, my family, and our future, so no matter what, I had to remain connected to my why while I navigated the emotions and reality of what was going on. This is incredibly important regardless of the magnitude of the situation you're facing. Always reconnect with your why and really evaluate what the residual impact will be. This applies to career moves and promotions, taking a leap of faith into entrepreneurship, or even starting over completely. Make sure you've done the work to think about where you are now versus where you are in the future and why this is important for your future self.

If you're facing a big decision or want to make a move, consider these questions:

- What's your why?
- What's your plan and timeline that will enable you to make an effective transition and handle all matters appropriately?
- How will you handle the conversations and mitigate issues so you can make moves with grace?
- What's the impact of this decision on others and how will you handle it?
- Are there any unintended consequences that need to be considered and how will you handle them?

Be mindful that growth is uncomfortable, change is uncomfortable, but nothing is as uncomfortable as staying stuck in a version of yourself that you've already outgrown. If you've hit a ceiling or feel as though your growth is stunted, consider what you can do to continue to evolve. Raise your hand when opportunities present themselves and make sure your desires are clear to advance or develop new skills and abilities. If entrepreneurship is your path, get crystal clear on the business you want to build and be honest as you progress. You are capable of amazing things, but those amazing things require the version of you that's committed to your next level to show up.

You're More Prepared Than You Think

If you've gotten to this point of the book, chances are you are wanting more, and my hope is that deep down inside you *believe* that the best is yet to come. As you continue to show up for yourself and lean into all of the areas of your life in which you can optimize, you will improve in ways that you can't even imagine. Making the daily commitment to yourself will unlock doors you can't even see yet, and my intention is that you adopt the mentality that the whole point of being alive is to evolve into the complete person you're intended to be. That evolution cannot transpire if you're holding yourself back, playing small, allowing your limiting beliefs to dictate your actions, or subscribing to a lack mentality. You were meant to shine bright, dream big, and achieve abundant success. Listen when I say that it doesn't happen by accident, or overnight, so you must commit to yourself, get clear about what you want, and make the moves you need to make in order to optimize your potential.

Thinking about what's possible for you should excite you, and it's totally okay if it makes you nervous as well. In fact, I would challenge you to think bigger if the thoughts of your next-level dreams do not scare you. Believe in the fact that you were born

> *It's up to* you *and only you to maximize your impact and leave a legacy that you're proud of.*

with unique talents, strengths, and abilities but it's up to *you* and only you to maximize your impact and leave a legacy that you're proud of. I encourage you to ruthlessly audit your life, career, and vision to make sure you're not stunting your own growth by staying stuck in a version of yourself that you've already outgrown. Trust me when I say that if you truly commit to showing up daily for yourself, focus on incremental improvements, and refuse to quit, your life and career can and will look completely different six months from now.

As a recap, here are a few reminders:

- Visualize what you want your life to be like and how you want to feel.

- Get really clear about your emotions and where you are at this stage of life.

- Identify any cognitive distortions that are clouding your judgment or affecting your behavior.

- Surround yourself with support from people who have your best interest at heart and can give you applicable and appropriate advice.

- Take your time to evaluate your current situation and do not make emotional decisions.

- Pray, meditate, and focus daily on what you want your life to look and feel like.

- Be grateful for every step on your journey and allow that to emanate as you either lean in more where you are or transition to new opportunities.

- Honor yourself, first, and never apologize for wanting more.

- Remember that self-awareness is the key to being remarkable as the leader of your life.

It's especially important to love yourself, even more, when you're going through a significant change. You're evolving, healing, growing, and discovering yourself all over again and in a whole new light. Trust that the discomfort will disappear over time as you truly step into your power and take ownership of the next-level version of yourself. Most important, when you're given an opportunity to change your life for the better, do it.

In addition to the questions and prompts throughout this chapter, I encourage you to leverage this final framework as a guide for you as you lean into what's next. Meant for M.O.R.E.

framework (Figure 10.1) is designed for those who are ready for more, whether it's personally or professionally, and will enable you to define what it is you want and create a plan on how to secure new opportunities for your future. It combines many of the principles and topics covered throughout this book, and my hope is that it becomes a useful resource for you whenever you're ready to level up. You can also download this from www .shebelievedbook.com/resources.

As I type these final words to you, my child continues to recover, the dust has begun to settle, and I am beyond grateful for my next chapter. I've continued to surround myself with support and have welcomed amazing new friends and mentors into my life as I continue to grow and level up each and every day.

My hope is that if you're ready to make the daily commitment to yourself that you deserve, you do the same. Trust that the calling in your heart was placed there for a reason, even if others don't fully understand it. Take action and believe that you're prepared

MINDSET	OPPORTUNITIES
Are you ready to lean in and evolve? Is your mindset currently limiting you? What thoughts need to be addressed?	What opportunities do you want to pursue or create for yourself personally and professionally?

ROAD MAP	EXECUTE
What's your game plan? Create small steps, goals, or micro-commitments that will help you achieve your overall goal.	Start doing the work. Makes moves. Track your progress. Commit to your next level!

FIGURE 10.1   Meant for M.O.R.E. framework.

for such a time as this. Don't get overwhelmed; rather, make a plan and lean into the discomfort of the unknown with the faith that you're being guided and supported every step of the way. Get excited about what it means for your future self and trust that the best is yet to come.

Remember that I believe in you 1,000% and my goal is that you do, too.

You've got this and I will forever be cheering you on. Remember that I believe in you 1,000% and my goal is that you do, too. The world needs you, and never forget that you deserve abundant success and are fully capable of creating the life you can't stop thinking about. Give yourself permission to evolve into the next version of yourself and trust that you can accomplish anything you set your mind to. Thank you for being here, showing up for yourself, doing the work, and committing to your future. Here's to recognizing your potential each and every day and leaning into the magic that is you. After all, you've already got what it takes.

Acknowledgments

My heart is full of gratitude for all of the incredible people who have influenced and shaped me into the woman I am today. This is by no means an exhaustive list, but I would be remiss if I didn't share my appreciation and love for those that have been a special part of this journey.

My husband, Brian Walsh, for always being my rock and believing in my ability to do anything I set my mind to.

My incredible kids, Madison, Brooklyn, and Bradley. Thank you for being my why and inspiring me each and every day.

Mom and Dad, thank you for always supporting my *big* dreams and goals, and being an instrumental part of our lives day in and day out.

Grams, you were a massive influence on my life and I miss you daily. Thank you for believing in me when I did not.

Elise Kashmiry, Melissa Dobies Kroon, and Megan Noha, I can't thank you enough for our decades of friendship. You are gifts in my life.

Jennifer McKenna, my partner in crime, I love you dearly. Our McKenna Walsh days always have been and forever will be some of my favorite memories.

Johanna Kandel, I am so glad you faxed me in 2006! You are a remarkable person and I am so honored to be championing the fight against eating disorders with you.

Brian Schweitzer, aka my "chief unicorn," you are, and forever will be, a very special person in my life. Thank you for always being there.

Ana Yebba, thank you for always being a part of my life. You have been a true friend, and have experienced and hosted so many of the most important moments of my life. Thank you!

The Leclerc Family, thank you for being there through all of the ups and downs, especially on my quest to the crown. You're so special to me and I am grateful for your friendship.

To my Allison Walsh Consulting team, you are all total *queens*! I absolutely *love* that we get to create magic together. I love, adore, and thank God for each of you every day!

My clients! I can't believe I have been so blessed to not only work with you but also call you dear friends. I am so proud of you and the work that's been done. What's even better is that I know it's just the beginning. Each of you are absolutely amazing and I am honored to have been on this journey with you.

To the amazing She Believed She Could community, you inspire me daily! Thank you for continuing to show up for *yourself* and committing to optimizing your growth and potential.

The Miss Florida Scholarship Program, you changed my life in the most incredible way. I will forever be grateful for the opportunity to have served as Miss Florida 2006, and I have loved being involved ever since. Thank you from the bottom of my heart for shaping me into the strong, resilient, and dedicated woman I am today.

Cynthia Johnson, there aren't enough words to thank you. Your friendship and guidance are priceless. Thank you for running alongside me and helping me to see opportunities that I never knew existed.

Beth Maynard, I knew you were amazing the moment we met but I had no idea the depth of the relationship that would be formed. Thank you for everything.

Kristen Hartnagel, your guidance, and support made this book come to life. You were able to extract exactly what needed to be shared. Thank you!

Niyc Pidgeon and Mel Deague, you changed my life. I needed positive psychology more than I realized! Thank you for pouring into me so I could help others along my path, too. The ripple effect is real!

Dr. Laura Gallaher, you helped me navigate through some of the most difficult and challenging situations and taught me how to be a better leader each and every day. I will be forever grateful.

Sandee Nebel, your friendship and guidance were pivotal at so many moments. Thank you for helping me step with clarity into the next chapter.

Lynn Grefe, you inspired me in more ways than you'll ever know. I miss you and try to emulate your impact with my own mentees daily.

Lisa Maile, thank you for helping me find my voice and use it at such an early age. Your belief in me changed the trajectory of my life and I will be forever grateful.

Joyce Perrone, thank you for instilling in me the ability to set and achieve goals at a young age. What you encouraged me to do has been shared with millions!

Jeb Blount, thank you for helping to make my book dream come true! I am so grateful for all of the doors you opened and the opportunities you've given me.

To the Wiley team, thank you for this incredible opportunity. I have wanted to write a book since I was 18 years old and that dream came true because of you. Here's to many more!

Sally Baker, thank you for seeing my vision and believing in the potential of this book. You were instrumental in this dream becoming a reality. Thank you!

Christina Verigan, you are an editing queen! Thank you for helping me best represent myself in words and sharing your expertise with me.

Advanced Recovery Systems, there are not enough words to express my appreciation for the beautiful career I was privileged to experience. Thank you for believing in me and giving me the opportunity to learn, grow, fail, and succeed. And to my team, you are *legendary*! Thank you for being phenomenal people who I will forever cheer for.

Charlie Health, wow! What an amazing team and mission! I am thrilled to propel us forward for years to come! Carter, Justin, and Caroline, thank you for the opportunity to serve and run alongside you as we work to help more kids get better, faster. I can't wait to change the world with you.

And last to all of my friends, cheerleaders, and supporters who have been there through the ups and downs, and the messy and the magical seasons of life. I love you and appreciate you more than you know.

About the Author

Allison Walsh, JD, is an expert business consultant, international speaker, and influential leader. By age 30, Allison became the vice president of Advanced Recovery Systems, a company destined for unicorn status, which she helped build from the ground up. She was also instrumental in the creation of Nobu, a mental wellness app, increasing access to mental health resources and support nationwide. Allison continues to contribute her expertise to meaningful, mission-driven companies within the behavioral health care industry including Charlie Health, a rapidly growing virtual mental health company focused on ending youth suicide.

Allison writes for and is featured in many media outlets including *Forbes, Entrepreneur, Fortune, Harvard Business Review, Nasdaq, Business Insider, Bustle*, and more, often collaborating with global mental health experts, influencers, and content creators. She commands the stage as a sought-after speaker who, beginning at the age of 18, has inspired international audience members numbering over 200,000. Named in the *Orlando Business Journal's* 2021 Top 40 Under 40 and Women Who Mean Business, Allison is a proud member of Forbes Business Development Council, Entrepreneur Leadership Network, and *Orlando Business Journal's* Leadership Trust.

Allison has won multiple awards for her philanthropy, raising over \$2 million for eating disorders prevention and awareness, and serves on numerous nonprofit boards. Having previously been crowned Miss Florida 2006, she's passionate about the advancement of women in leadership, which fueled her desire to create the She Believed She Could Podcast and found Allison Walsh Consulting. Through the creation of her coaching programs, workbooks, and curriculum she's been able to improve the mindset, confidence, personal branding, and communications skills of a roster of over 300 clients, and thousands more in her online community. Allison draws from her expertise in positive psychology, the science of happiness, well-being, and success to provide women with tools for advancement both personally and professionally. As a business development, marketing, and personal branding expert, Allison is on a mission to help influential, high-stakes leaders build their confidence, grow their businesses, elevate their brands, and accomplish their goals. For more information, please visit www.allisonwalshconsulting.com.

Index